THE BRAIN TUMOUR THAT SAVED ME

An Ironwoman's Journey of Resilience, Humour, and Hope

Paula Johnson

LUCKY BOOK PUBLISHING

LUCKY BOOK PUBLISHING

Published by Lucky Book Publishing: LuckyBookPublishing.com

The author does not dispense medical advice or prescribe the use of any technique as a form of treatment for physical, emotional, or medical problems without the advice of a physician, either directly or indirectly. The intent of the author is only to offer information of a general true nature to help you in your quest for emotional, physical and spiritual well-being. In the event you use any of the information in this book for yourself, the author and the publisher assume no responsibility for your actions.

Some names, identifying details, and circumstances in this book have been changed to protect the privacy of those involved.

To request permissions, contact the publisher at

hello@luckybookpublishing.com.

For speaking opportunities and coaching inquiries, visit

www.paulastories.com

Paperback ISBN: 978-1-997775-62-1
Hardcover ISBN: 978-1-997775-61-4
E-book ISBN: 978-1-997775-60-7

First edition, March 2026

MY GIFT TO YOU

I am so glad you're here!

As my gift to you, get FREE Access to the Audiobook of

The Brain Tumour That Saved Me and other bonus content by scanning the QR Code below or visiting

http://paulastories.com

Preface

If you had told me years ago that a brain tumour would change my life for the better, I wouldn't have believed you. But here we are.

For much of my life, I believed resilience was something you either had or you didn't, reserved for the strong and extraordinary, not for ordinary people muddling through life. I thought you had to be fearless before you started, certain before you leapt, healed before you tried again.

Life, of course, had other plans.

This book navigates life's detours, disasters, miracles, and moments of ridiculousness, and what they reveal when the adrenaline fades. It traces the quiet work of accepting help, discovering community, and finding laughter where you least expect it.

It's not a manual for survival, a guide to becoming an Ironwoman, or a prescription for turning pain into punchlines. It's simply my story: honest, unfinished, and shared with as much hope as I can muster.

Each chapter shares a piece of my story, followed by reflections and questions for you. You're welcome to pause and explore them, or simply turn the page and stay with the story. This journey is yours, too.

I've wanted to write this book for many years. Now that it's finally here, I feel relieved, grateful, and, truthfully, a little terrified to release it into the world. Sharing these words feels more vulnerable than any race I've ever started.

I hope it lands where you need it most.

If you're reading this, I hope you find a little of your own story here too.

The Dream

My dream for this book is simple.

I hope someone finds it on a day when life feels heavier than usual. A day when they're tired of being strong. A day when they're wondering if they're behind, broken, too much, not enough, or somehow doing life wrong.

This isn't about winning races, surviving diagnoses, or collecting dramatic plot twists like race medals. It's about what happens after. It's about the moments when you're left sitting quietly with yourself, wondering who you are now, and whether you're allowed to want more.

I want this book to remind you that resilience isn't something you're born with; it's something you build quietly. Surviving is not the same as believing in yourself. Many of us prove we're capable long before we ever trust ourselves.

Let this book make room for doubt, fear, grief, laughter, rage, rest, and beginning again.

If triathlon taught me anything, it's this: you don't have to feel ready to begin. That lesson applies far beyond sport: to healing, reinvention, community, creativity, love, and the quiet decision to trust yourself, one small step at a time.

If something here resonates, please pass it along: to a friend, a sister, a colleague, or someone standing at the edge of their own beginning. Stories like this only matter if they travel.

Most of all, I want to plant a gentle but stubborn thought in your mind: If she can survive this imperfectly, humorously, messily, maybe I can too.

And maybe the thing you fear will break you isn't the end of your story.

Maybe it's the beginning of a chapter you don't yet understand.

That's my dream.

Dedication

For my mother.

For your strength.

For your resilience.

For your love: steady, unspoken, and unwavering.

Everything I have done, every hard thing I have survived, every finish line I have crossed, happened because of your support. I hope I have made you proud.

Contents

Chapter 1
The Best Brain Tumour Ever

The body whispers long before it demands to be heard.
I just didn't know yet what it was trying to tell me.

It started with a shocking, searing pain right between my eyes that almost brought me to my knees. At the time, I thought it was stress.

It was December 22nd, a Christmas shopping day. My family was 3,000 miles away in England, so, once again, the presents would be late. With my usual urgency, I rushed to a department store, determined to get it done.

And, as one does when Christmas shopping for others, I panicked and started looking at things for myself.

I picked up a beautiful espresso machine. That's when it hit. A lightning bolt of pain, straight between my eyes. I almost dropped the box.

Placing it back on the shelf, I thought maybe it was a *sign* not to spend the money. I moved on, found a few gifts for my mum and sister, and headed to the checkout. Just as I was about to pay, the pain struck again. So intense that I had to lean my forehead on the counter to stop from collapsing.

The cashier stared at me, alarmed. “Are you okay?”

Mortified, I muttered, “I’m fine. Just stress.”

That night, the stabbing sensation came and went, waking me repeatedly. I chalked it up to a migraine or holiday stress, the kind of thing nurses tend to diagnose themselves with.

A Nurse Who Became the Patient

The next morning, I went to work as a diabetes research nurse. A pregnant patient was scheduled for 7 a.m., and because I was the only one assigned to the clinic that early, cancelling wasn’t an option.

During her visit, she casually mentioned that she was being monitored for a pituitary tumour. It was benign, she said, but her endocrinologist wanted to watch it closely during pregnancy.

I remember nodding, offering reassurance, and thinking how frightening that must feel.

I had no idea how close to home that story was about to become.

When she left, I wandered to the emergency department. I almost didn’t go in, convinced they’d roll their eyes and tell me to take a seat. I’d begun to wonder if maybe I *was* a hypochondriac.

For years, I’d been healthy and athletic, even competing in Ironman triathlons, yet riddled with strange symptoms no one could diagnose. Every specialist I was referred to treated their own piece of the puzzle, and a few even implied it was all in my head.

This time, though, something was different. The triage nurse seemed concerned and immediately brought me into a room. Within minutes, I was being rushed through tests: a CT scan, blood work, and an ECG.

After four hours, guilt crept in. *They're spending all this time on me, and it's probably nothing.*

Then the senior doctor walked in with a serious look on his face.

"Paula," he said gently, "you have a mass in your brain, on your pituitary gland."

The world didn't shatter the way I expected it to.

It went strangely quiet.

It was as if I were watching a scene from a movie I hadn't auditioned for, certain someone would eventually yell "cut" and send me back to my real life.

My first emotion wasn't fear. It was relief. I wasn't a hypochondriac after all. My body had been telling the truth. I had known for a few years that something was wrong, but no one was listening.

There was fear, yes, but it arrived later, in waves.

The doctor explained, "Because of the tumour, you have diabetes and an enlarged heart. And your joint pain? That's arthritis, because your bones are actively growing."

I half-laughed, half-cried. "Is there anything else?"

He added softly, "We'll refer you to an endocrinologist and a neurosurgeon. You have a rare condition, but it's treatable."

Treatable. That word became my lifeline. I clung to it, because everything else suddenly felt like it was sliding.

Diagnosis and Denial

Of course, the first thing I did when I got home was open my computer. I typed *pituitary tumour – acromegaly.*

The first images that appeared were André the Giant, Lurch from *The Addams Family*, and faces with exaggerated, coarse features. I was actually slowly growing, inside and out, in my late thirties. My stomach turned.

Was this what Jake saw when he looked at me?

What everyone saw?

What I'd been slowly becoming without knowing?

What if the treatment didn't work?

As I continued reading, I learned about the other serious health consequences caused by the tumour pressing on my pituitary gland and producing excess growth hormone: high blood pressure, life-threatening heart issues, and an increased risk of breast, thyroid, and colon cancers. For more on this diagnosis, see Appendix A.

The moment Jake came home, he saw me sitting there, staring at the computer screen, tears streaming down my face. We'd only been married for five months.

My voice shook as I told him everything.

"Jake," I said, "what did you ever see in me? You married a monster."

I meant it. In that moment, I couldn't see past the diagnosis or the distorted images on the screen. I couldn't see myself at all.

Without missing a beat, he grinned, his tone reassuring.

"Paula, Paula, Paula... I didn't marry you for your looks. I married you for your money."

The Irony of Working Beside Your Diagnosis

Soon after, I was referred to one of Canada's top experts in this rare condition, Dr. Shereen Ezzat. The irony bordered on absurdity. He worked in the same department, just a few offices away.

The day before my diagnosis, I attended a lunchtime lecture on this very condition, its rarity, its subtle presentation, and how notoriously difficult it was to diagnose. I sat listening intently, eating the free slice of pizza (the real reason I was there), never imagining I would be *that* rare patient. I was seated right beside him.

When he walked into the examination room the next day, fear caught me off guard. As a colleague, I'd always known him as intimidatingly brilliant, the kind of physician whose intellect filled the room. Sitting there in a blue hospital gown instead of scrubs, the role reversal was stark. I wasn't a nurse anymore.

For a brief moment, I felt reduced to a diagnosis, flattened into a clinical label rather than seen as the person behind it. The nurse who worked down the hall. The woman whose body had been quietly changing for years. Tears rose before I could stop them.

His expression softened. He reached for my hand.

“Paula,” he said gently, “we’re going to take good care of you. You are going to be okay.”

At that moment, the intimidating expert disappeared. What remained was a calm, deeply compassionate physician, a true patient advocate. I couldn’t have wished for a kinder or steadier doctor.

The clues rearranged themselves into clarity. The larger shoe size. The extra inch of height. The facial changes. The unexplained lactation. The exhaustion, joint pain, insatiable hunger, and widening gaps between my teeth.

It wasn’t *all in my head.*

It was in my head.

And the irony lingered: for years, I had worked beside my diagnosis, even learned about it, never knowing it was quietly shaping my life.

How many times had I missed the clues in myself?

The Waiting and the Worry

My neurosurgeon, Dr. Fred Gentili, was world-renowned for operating on these types of tumours, which only three in a million people are diagnosed with each year. Our house was only five kilometres away from that hospital.

The pain I’d felt was caused by the tumour hemorrhaging, it was too large for surgery. So, for three months, I had to inject myself three times daily with medication to stop its growth and the bleeding.

I'd given hundreds of injections to others. I was hopeless at giving them to myself. My hands shook every time. "I can't do it!"

Jake offered to help. I told him, "You haven't even practiced on an orange!" So, he did. And then he helped me every day. My colleagues even took turns when I couldn't.

The Surgery

The day before surgery, I hugged every colleague and told them I'd loved working with them, just in case I didn't make it. I called my family in England, holding back tears as I reassured them I'd be fine. They'd sent me a video of good-luck messages, but I was so emotional I couldn't bring myself to watch it.

When I met with Dr. Gentili, my only question was, "When can I swim, bike, and run again?" (A reasonable question. I'd been obsessed with triathlon for six years.)

He raised his eyebrows. "My dear, I'm not sure you'll want to be doing that after surgery."

He clearly didn't know me.

As the gurney rolled toward the operating room, my mind did what minds do best under threat: catastrophize at Olympic speed.

What if I didn't wake up? What if I reacted to the anesthetic? What if I lost the strength and endurance I'd built over the last few years?

What if Dr. Gentili sneezed mid-surgery?

Then someone placed a mask over my face and told me

to take deep breaths. The questions loosened their grip. The ceiling lights blurred. I remember thinking, briefly and irrationally, that this felt like the moment just before the gun goes off.

And then there was nothing at all.

The transsphenoidal surgery involved going through my nose and sinus tract, followed by drilling a hole into my skull. It was supposed to take two and a half hours. Jake waited anxiously, as he watched the clock: three, four, then five hours went by. After five and a half hours, Dr. Gentili finally walked out, beads of sweat on his forehead. "Your wife is fine," he said. "She just has an exceedingly thick skull."

To which my husband replied, "I could have told you that!"

Recovery and Resilience

When I woke up in the ICU a few hours later, the bright lights hurt my eyes. I was surrounded by tubes, monitors, and beeping machines. The first thing I remember is being ravenously hungry. "I'm starving," I blurted.

The nurse hesitated and suggested ice chips would be more appropriate, but I was insistent. "I could eat a horse between two scabby mattresses."

I pleaded with her to bring me food, promising I had a very strong stomach. Reluctantly, she brought me a meal I will never forget: Salisbury steak, mashed potatoes, vegetables, and a smattering of gravy, the most divine hospital food I'd ever seen.

I devoured it.

...and promptly threw it up.

Recovery wasn't completely smooth. Three days after my surgery, I experienced a sudden and unbearable headache, which my nurse initially dismissed. When she asked me to rate the pain on a scale of zero to ten, I responded, in agony, "Fourteen."

She said, "That's impossible. I just gave you pain medication. I need a number between zero and ten."

Meanwhile, the doctor seemed worried and sent me for an urgent CT scan. Fortunately, the scan was clear. He suggested the symptoms were likely due to inflammation that would resolve over time.

The stern nurse returned with a syringe full of pain medication and pushed it into my intravenous line. "This'll sort you out." There wasn't a glimmer of compassion in her tone.

A while later, she returned to check my vital signs. I could barely lift my arm; whatever the medication was, it was potent. Again, she asked me to rate the pain on a scale of zero to ten.

Exasperated, groggy, and a bit annoyed, I replied with a wry smile, "Minus four."

By the next morning, after a restless night, the pain was gone. Later, I accidentally vomited on the same nurse's shoes. I apologized, of course. Sort of.

The Ripple Effect

I didn't realize it then, but this tumour, my affectionately named "best brain tumour, ever," had been growing slowly for possibly six to eight years before diagnosis. It set off a chain of serendipitous events that would change not only my life but also potentially the lives of others.

This experience taught me how to listen, to trust, and to find laughter even when I was afraid. It also changed my understanding of what "strength" really means.

I had always believed strength meant pushing harder.

It would take time to understand that the tumour trying to undo me had been fuelling me and actually making me stronger.

Reflections

- I had been living in a body that was quietly changing. I didn't want to hear it.
- I had spent years apologizing for taking up space in exam rooms.
- Humour doesn't erase fear, but it can make it survivable.
- A diagnosis may change the story, but it doesn't define the person living it.

Questions to Sit With

- What has your body been trying to tell you that you keep negotiating with?
- What happens to your sense of identity when the roles you rely on suddenly shift?
- Has something you once labelled "the worst thing" ever turned out to carry an unexpected gift?

Chapter 2
Born Fighting – A Premature Beginning

Some of us enter the world quietly. Others arrive fighting.

It's strange, looking back. The first time my life hung in the balance, I was too small to remember it. The second time, I was old enough to fear it.

From the moment I arrived, I seemed determined to make life difficult. My entrance into the world was dramatic, messy, and, in hindsight, almost suspiciously on brand for how the rest of my life would unfold.

December 1966. My mum was 30 weeks pregnant with me when everything changed. My parents lived in a remote village called Butteryhaugh in northern England, tucked deep in a vast forest near the Scottish border. Dad was a lumberjack, so they moved there to be closer to his work. The village was small, maybe 30 houses, a wooden church that looked more like a shack, and a community hall that doubled as the local school. There were no shops, but a grocery truck rolled in twice a week, which was as close to "town life" as we got.

Everyone knew everyone, and privacy was more of a polite

suggestion than a reality. News travelled faster than the mail, and if something happened to you, three people knew before you finished your tea.

One early morning, Mum was jolted awake by frantic banging on the front door. Everyone in the village knew she was a nurse, so people often came knocking for advice or help. Half-asleep, she hurried to answer, but her heavy, pregnant belly threw her off balance. She slipped and tumbled down the stairs.

The banging at the door turned out to be the mother of the boy next door. Her son was trying to fake another illness to skip school. But this time, Mum had become the real emergency. She was in severe pain and was rushed by ambulance to the hospital in Hexham, an hour's drive away through winding forest roads.

The doctors decided on an emergency forceps delivery. I was born tiny, blue, and weak, whisked away to an incubator before my mum could even hold me. A few hours later, a nurse gently woke her with heartbreaking words a mother should never hear.

"Your baby might not make it through the night."

She asked if Mum had a name for me so I could be baptized. She hadn't decided yet, as she'd been expecting a boy named *Paul*. So, in her dazed state, she said, "Paula."

Coincidentally, *Paula* means *small*, and I certainly lived up to that name, for a while anyway.

I survived the night, barely, but that was the first of many fights.

Days later, I was transferred to the neonatal unit in Newcastle, 80 kilometres (50 miles) away. The doctors told my parents I might survive but warned that I would likely be "stunted," under five feet tall, and "mentally retarded," as the cruel language of the time went. After a month in that incubator, I didn't just survive. I thrived.

A year later, my sister, Maria, was born. A few months later, we moved from Butteryhaugh to a place called Washington New Town, where my dad was starting a new career.

Mum often tells me a story from those early days. When I was around two years old, she was pushing me in my stroller shortly after we'd arrived in Washington, and as people walked toward us, my little face lit up, ready. In Butteryhaugh, everyone knew everyone. Strangers weren't strangers; they were future hellos.

But this time, no one stopped. No smiles. No greetings. They just walked past.

Mum said she watched my smile slowly fade, confusion giving way to disappointment, as if I couldn't quite understand how a world could exist where people didn't acknowledge each other.

Apparently, that moment stuck.

To this day, I still smile at strangers. And yes, I'll admit it, I still feel a wave of disappointment when they don't smile back. But when they do? It feels like a small, shared win. A moment of connection. A reminder that being seen matters.

Mind you, it's also gotten me into trouble once or twice... so I do try to be a bit more selective now.

Those early years taught me that the world could be kind, that people would smile back if you smiled first. But school didn't always follow the same rules.

When I was four, our family moved from Washington to Durham City, with another addition, my brother, David. It should have felt like a fresh start, but instead it marked the beginning of a much harder chapter.

Cruel Classrooms and Small Victories

Sadly, my school days were darkened by some less-than-supportive teachers.

One in particular, Mrs. Tomas, terrified me. She was a tall, heavyset woman with a permanently etched, angry expression. I would lie awake at night, worrying about her class the next day, my stomach twisted with dread.

I was eight years old when, one day, during a math test, I couldn't remember where I'd left off the day before. I raised my hand and asked timidly, "Miss, where do I start?"

Without hesitation, she grabbed my arm with one hand and began *slapping the backs of my legs and bum*, singing mockingly, "Start at the very beginning..." from *The Sound of Music.*

The sting of her palm was equal to the sting of humiliation.

When I got home, I told Mum everything. She was furious. The next day, she marched me to school and demanded to see the headmaster, showing him the finger-shaped bruises on the back of my legs. She insisted that I be moved from that woman's class. I don't know if Mrs. Tomas was ever punished, but I was moved into the *remedial class*.

At first, it felt like another humiliation. But I soon realized something unexpected: I was actually top of the class there. For the first time, I wasn't at the bottom, struggling to keep up. I started to feel a tiny spark of confidence.

Growing Pains

By the time I was fourteen, I was the opposite of what they predicted: tall, overweight, and a little accident-prone, but certainly *not* "stunted." I'd even shot past average height. Unfortunately, my feet had followed suit.

Much to my dismay, I wore a CAN/US size 11 (UK size 9) shoe. I still remember going to shoe stores with Mum and leaving in tears because the only pair that fit were always the ugliest on the rack. If you'd asked me then, "Paula, what's the worst thing that could happen to you?" I'd probably have said, "My feet getting any bigger."

High school wasn't much kinder. I dreaded Phys Ed, and my teacher seemed to take pleasure in humiliating me.

"Paula Johnson, you're a lump of lard, and you'll never amount to anything," she sneered in front of the whole class.

Everyone laughed. I just wanted to melt into the shadows of the gym and disappear. Her words didn't just hurt. They settled inside me like wet cement, cold, heavy, and hardening into a belief I'd carry for years. The shame stayed with me for a long time.

A New Beginning

I struggled through junior and senior school, always having to work twice as hard just to keep pace. But I made it through, bruised, maybe, but not broken.

College and Nursing School were a turning point. All I ever wanted to be was a nurse, following in my mother's footsteps. I finally found a place where kindness mattered as much as intelligence, where empathy was valued over appearance. It felt like home, the kind of place where the girl who'd once been told she'd "never amount to anything" could finally start proving everyone wrong.

What I didn't know then was that finishing school wasn't the end of my fight; it was the start of becoming the version of myself I'd always imagined.

The fragile, premature baby they said might not survive... survived. The awkward schoolgirl who felt like she was always catching up... caught up.

For the first time, I began to believe I might be meant for more than surviving. Maybe I was meant to explore, to risk, to leap.

So, when adulthood arrived, loudly and without warning, I embraced it the only way I knew how: with stubbornness, hope, and a ridiculous amount of determination.

Eventually, that determination pushed me toward the biggest leap of all.

A leap across an ocean.

Reflections

- Survival is its own kind of strength, even when it arrives quietly or imperfectly.
- Words spoken early can wound deeply, but they don't get the final say.
- Kindness leaves marks, too—often stronger ones.
- The traits we struggle with most are often the ones that make us unmistakably ourselves.
- Beginnings matter, but they do not dictate endings.

Questions Worth Sitting With

- When were you first told, directly or indirectly, that you "couldn't"?
- How have early experiences shaped the way you see your own strength today?
- Whose words have lingered longest in your life, and which ones are you ready to release?
- What part of yourself have you tried to shrink or hide, and what if it's actually a source of power?
- Where could you offer kindness now, in the way someone once offered it to you?

Chapter 3
Tri-ing to Live – At Least She Tri'd

I didn't change my life because I felt ready.
I changed it because I couldn't stay the same.

In 1990, I moved from England to Toronto, Canada. I'd dreamed of it since my teens, after visiting family on the East Coast and falling in love with the vastness, the ocean air, the endless horizons, and the sense that life could be bigger. On that same trip, we visited Boston. Standing beneath its skyscrapers, I felt it instantly: the pull of a big city, alive with energy and possibility. Somewhere between the open Atlantic and those towering buildings, I knew I wanted more.

Nurse recruiters from Toronto had come to London, dangling a tempting offer in front of hundreds of us: Come, work in Canada. We'll pay your flight, double your NHS salary, and give you a fresh start.

I jumped.

They greeted us at Pearson International Airport with baskets of apples and muffins, waving Canadian flags like we were celebrities. It was the most wholesome recruitment scheme I'd ever seen.

Although vastly different from New Brunswick, where I'd

originally "fallen in love" with Canada, Toronto carried the same big-city pulse I'd felt in Boston: busy, bold, and brimming with possibility. I landed a job as a registered nurse on the Thoracic and Respirology unit at the highly respected Toronto General Hospital.

I learned so much there, about lungs, life, and how to function on very little sleep. But in the late '90s, government cutbacks and layoffs swept through, and I had to find a new position.

I didn't know it then, but that loss would quietly nudge me toward the start line of a very different life.

June 1999: The Breakup, the Breakdown, and the Beginning

By 1999, I was working as a nurse in a sports injury clinic. It was mid-June. Outside, the city was bursting with sunshine; inside, I was quietly falling apart.

I'd just found out my boyfriend was cheating on me.

We'd only been dating for three months, but I'd already written the soundtrack in my head. His name was Paul; my name was Paula. There's literally a song about us. In my mind, this was a sign from the universe.

Apparently, the universe disagreed.

The breakup slid neatly into my long-standing narrative of low self-worth. Of course he cheated. I was never going to be enough. The words of my old Phys Ed teacher echoed inside my head like a bad remix:

"You're a lump of lard, Paula Johnson. You are never going to amount to anything."

Glancing down at myself, I weighed around 250 pounds. I was unhappy and unhealthy, and this was not the life I imagined when I left England with a head full of hopes and dreams.

I can't keep living like this. I felt so lonely. So ashamed.

Something had to change.

I picked up the phone and called Paul. He didn't answer, so I left a message, tears rolling down my cheeks.

"Hey, Paul, it's Paula. I thought we had something really special, but now I think you're just a big hairy liar. Goodbye."

I hung up, feeling breathless and numb. I wiped my eyes and took a shaky breath.

At that moment, a woman walked into the clinic, clutching her knee. I muttered something about allergies as I tried to pull myself together.

With a tone of desperation, she said, "I need to see the doctor. I'm doing a triathlon in seven weeks, and I've hurt my knee."

While she waited, my curiosity outweighed my heartbreak.

"What's a triathlon?" I asked.

"It's a race with a swim, bike, and run," she said. "It's fun."

She looked... normal, not like the superhuman athletes I'd seen on TV.

"Wow. You do that? I've seen it on TV, people nearly drowning, crawling over the finish line..."

She laughed. "Oh no, that's the Ironman. That's a longer, completely crazy race. The one I'm doing is just a 750-metre swim, 30-kilometre bike, and a seven-kilometre run."

"Just," she said.

But something in me sparked.

Even though I hadn't swum or run in over 20 years, a thought bubbled up.

I could do that.

It was a small, reckless idea and definitely out of character.

It was also the first flicker of self-belief I'd felt in a very long time.

The First Swim

(also known as: The Lifeguard Incident)

That evening, buoyed by utter ignorance and a moment of bravado, I went to the pool for my first swim in years.

I almost drowned.

I made it one length, maybe less, before the world closed in. The lifeguard had to haul me out and put me in the recovery position on the pool deck. Not my finest moment.

As I lay there, trying to cling to my dignity and my last lungful of air, he said kindly, "You weren't breathing."

"Was I dead?" I asked, horrified.

He laughed. "No, you just tried to swim without lifting your head to breathe. You've got to breathe periodically."

A basic, but important detail.

He gave me a few simple tips: "As you lift your elbow and bring your hand forward, turn your head to the side and breathe into your armpit."

Not quite Olympic-level coaching, but it was a start.

Embarrassed but stubborn, I went back the next night. And the night after that. I refused to let a near-drowning experience end my attempt at a triathlon.

The following evening, feeling wildly optimistic, I dug out an old pair of tennis shoes and went for my first run in 20 years.

I ran like the wind... for about half a block.

Then I collapsed, wheezing, and basically crawled home.

The next day, every muscle in my body ached.

Learning How Not to Die While Training

I shuffled into the sports injury physician's office where I worked and told him, somewhat proudly, that I was training for a triathlon.

He looked at my worn-out tennis shoes as if they were evidence in a crime.

"First," he said, "get rid of those and buy proper running shoes."

Then he explained a plan that didn't involve my heart exploding.

"Run for one minute, walk for one minute. Repeat that ten times. In a few days, try a two-minute run, one-minute walk. Next week, try a three-minute run, one-minute walk. Eventually, aim for a ten-minute run, one-minute walk. And keep going."

It sounded both simple and impossible.

But it was good advice.

I didn't quite make it to the 10-and-1 stage before race day, but seven weeks after my breakup, I stood on the start line of the same triathlon my patient was doing.

I borrowed a wetsuit from a friend and squeezed into it like a sausage casing. I bought a bike from one of my colleagues, an old red steel-framed beauty that had been hanging in his garage for 15 years. I named her Rocket.

She was ancient but sturdy, and I loved her.

Since I didn't have a car, my friend Suzanne drove us up to Orillia, north of Toronto. I'd done a bit of panicked internet research on "how to do a triathlon," but honestly, I had no idea what I was getting myself into.

My plan was… well, not so much a plan as a vague intention: swim, bike, run as hard as possible until either I crossed the finish line or collapsed trying.

I was still overweight but had lost a few pounds during the seven weeks of training, which felt like a miracle.

We got there an hour before the race. I was a bit excited but mostly terrified. I set up my bike and running gear in the transition area. While I tried to figure out what to do next, some of the other women in the race admired my bike.

"She's gorgeous," they said.

I beamed. In retrospect, they were probably admiring how *retro* she was, since most of them had sleek aluminium or carbon-fibre machines. But Rocket and I didn't care. We were just happy to be there.

The Race

The swim was terrifying.

I had only ever swum in a pool before. This was open water, a large lake that seemed to stretch to infinity. Thankfully, it was fairly shallow, and I could see the bottom most of the way, which helped somewhat, but not enough to convince me I wasn't about to drown again.

The borrowed wetsuit was at least two sizes too small and felt like it was trying to strangle me. I spent much of the swim using breaststroke, partly because I was afraid to put my face in the water, and partly because I physically couldn't breathe.

Halfway through, I stopped, ripped the zipper down, and essentially turned the wetsuit into a useless neoprene cape. But I could breathe.

Somehow, I made it to shore, staggered out of the lake, and shuffled the 300 metres to transition. Wrestling off the wetsuit was a race in itself. I peeled it off and dried my feet. Pulled on my shorts and running shoes. Clipped on my helmet and hopped onto Rocket.

Once I was on the bike, something shifted instantly.

On the bike, I came alive.

I started passing people who had sailed past me in the swim. The course was hilly, but what went up came down. I flew down the descents, grinning like a maniac. For the first time, I felt powerful.

Before I knew it, I was back in transition, wobbling out on legs that felt like jelly, ready (sort of) to run.

As I shuffled out, I saw a woman sprinting toward the finish line. She was about to win the race, yet when she saw me awkwardly hobbling onto the run course, she slowed just enough to shout:

“You’ve got this! Go, go, go, you can do this!”

This woman took the time to encourage a complete newbie who still smelled like lake water and panic.

Later, I learned her name: Lisa Bentley. An incredible athlete who, at 20, had been diagnosed with cystic fibrosis, a disease that often dramatically affects quality and length of life... and yet she went on to win 11 full Ironman races.

As I began my seven-kilometre run, Lisa was crossing the finish line.

I was inspired. I was also mildly horrified.

She was *done*, and I was just about to start.

But I started anyway.

And that was when I realized something profound:

I hated running.

Despite dreading every step, I loved who I was becoming.

I finished that race. I wasn't first, but I was nowhere near last. That day, I won something far more important than a medal.

For the first time I could remember, I believed in myself.

Crossing that finish line wasn't about the distance.

I didn't know who I was becoming yet.

I just knew I didn't want to go back.

Triathlon, Tumour... Superpowers?

Years later, I'd look back and wonder about that "sudden spark of inspiration" in the sports injury clinic, the one that compelled me, out of nowhere, to sign up for a triathlon.

I had no idea that back then, I had a rare tumour that was causing me to naturally produce abnormally high levels of growth hormone. Athletes have been known to illegally inject themselves with growth hormone to enhance their performance. My body had been quietly changing for years. Energy surges. Increasing strength. An inch taller. Feet growing, longer and wider. In my thirties.

I didn't know my body was already rewriting the rules.

At the time, all I knew was that I had energy to burn, muscles that seemed to grow faster than my budget for sports gear, and a drive that bordered on obsessiveness.

Instead of questioning it, I did something new for me. When life handed me extra fuel:

I pushed harder.

Went faster.

Aimed higher.

And that's how I stumbled, quite enthusiastically, into the next chapter of my life. A chapter fuelled by adrenaline, community, and some questionable decisions.

Reflections

- Action has a way of rewriting the stories we've told ourselves for years.
- You don't have to feel ready or confident to begin. Movement creates belief, not the other way around.
- Finding your people changes everything. Belonging turns effort into joy.

Questions to Take With You

- What old label or criticism have you been carrying that no longer deserves your loyalty?
- What's one small, imperfect step you could take toward something that scares you?
- Where might your own "tribe" be waiting, the people who would cheer simply because you showed up?

Chapter 4
The Luckiest St. Paddy's Day Race

I set out for a run.
Life took me somewhere else entirely.

March 2001. Back when I had energy to burn and no idea why, I signed up for the St. Patrick's Achilles 5K Run, one of my favourite events of the year.

The Achilles Track Club is an incredible non-profit that helps people of all abilities get out there and run, walk, or roll together. The remarkable club founder, Brian, is both hearing and visually impaired, yet he refuses to let these barriers stop him. The organization's big annual fundraiser is this race, and it's for such a great cause.

Even better? They serve *a* beer at the finish line. (Emphasis on *a*... as in one. Which, as you'll soon see, is an important distinction.)

It was one of those crisp March mornings when your lungs burn before you even start running, and every runner is bouncing around pretending it's *perfect weather* even though we're all freezing our arses off.

Anyone who's ever seen me race knows I like to keep things fun, especially in the last 100 metres. That's when I throw my arms up, wave them around, and hoot and holler as if I've just won the Boston Marathon. Mostly to entertain the crowd... but also because I'm about to collapse and I'm thrilled it's over. Plus, it makes for a great finish-line photo!

So, I crossed the line, arms flailing, face red, lungs on fire, and someone handed me a beer. It's Sunday morning, 10 a.m. (which is, for the record, 3 p.m. in Ireland, perfectly reasonable pint time).

I was thirsty. It was for charity. So, I chugged it.

Then a friend said, "I don't really want mine."

Well, I couldn't let *that* go to waste, right? Down it went.

Then another friend offered hers (she has celiac disease, so she can't tolerate it), and, you guessed it, I accepted.

There *may* have been a fourth beer, but I can neither confirm nor deny that.

It was 10:30 a.m. on a Sunday, and I've had three (possibly four) beers.

It was time to go home. I grabbed my knapsack and wobbled my way toward the subway.

Halfway home, I realized this was *not* one of my finer life choices. My stomach was staging a full protest. I stumbled off the train, praying for a public washroom, a garbage can, *anything*. Then I spotted a fancy new townhouse showroom, "The Bloor West Lofts." Jackpot! Surely they have a washroom.

I burst through the doors and was immediately greeted by an overly enthusiastic salesperson. "Welcome to The Bloor

West Lofts! Are you looking to buy a townhouse?"

"Not exactly," I gasped. "I'm looking for your *washroom*!"

He looked sympathetic but said, "Oh, sorry, the bathroom's just for show. It doesn't actually work."

Of course it doesn't.

I was about to leave, but then he said, "You don't look very well. Would you like some cheese and crackers?"

I declined the cheese but nibbled on a few crackers, starting to feel human again... and that's when things took a turn.

The next thing I know... I've eaten all of his crackers, and I'm signing papers. Apparently, between the crackers and the charm of the salesman's pitch, I decided that what my life really needed that Sunday morning, after a fun run and a few beers, was a *house*.

Several signatures and initials later, I stumbled back onto the subway, went home, and immediately passed out on the sofa.

Hours later, I woke up, groggy, and thought:

"Did I... just buy a house?"

Oh my God. What was I thinking? Can I even afford this? How many bedrooms? How many bathrooms? What did I *buy* exactly? Oh God! What have I done?

Cue the self-talk:

It's okay, Paula. You've wanted to buy for years. You can do this. You're responsible. You can totally handle this... right?

In an attempt to distract myself, I turned on the TV. The local news was on, covering the very same 5K race I ran that morning.

And then... there I was, on the news. Caught on camera sprinting to the finish line, arms flailing, whooping and cheering like a maniac.

The news announcer said, "Today was the St. Patrick's Day 5K, organized by the Achilles Track Club, helping people with disabilities participate in sport."

That's when it hit me: on national television, I appeared less "serious homeowner" and more "someone who probably shouldn't be signing contracts unsupervised."

Perfect. Just perfect.

Right then, the phone rang.

"Hello, is this Paula?"

"Yes..."

"Paula, we met this morning. I'm the real estate salesman. You bought the townhouse."

"Yes," I answered nervously.

"Did I just see you on the news?"

"Uh... maybe."

"Paula," he said cautiously,

"do you... have a parent or guardian who can help you sign for the house?"

I wanted the earth to swallow me whole.

"No! I'm fine. I'm an adult. Thank you. Goodbye!"

I could have backed out of the deal.

But I didn't. I bought the townhouse! Best. Drunken. Decision. Ever.

Actually, forget the "drunken" part. It was *hands down* the best decision of my life.

Somewhere between the crackers and the contract, I had unknowingly taken my first real step toward believing I deserved stability. That townhouse purchase was me, accidentally, choosing a future.

Twelve years later, on St. Patrick's Day, with the help of my real estate friend Jonathan, I sold that townhouse for a *very* nice profit.

So yes, I owe St. Patrick, the Achilles Track Club, and Steam Whistle beer a massive thank you.

Happy St. Paddy's Day, everyone. May your runs be fast, your beers cold, and your impulsive decisions just as lucky as mine. ☘️🍻

🍀 What I Learned (Somewhere Between the Finish Line and the Mortgage Papers)

- Sometimes the best decisions don't feel like decisions at all.
  You can analyze forever, but every now and then, a spontaneous "Why not?" quietly changes everything.
- I wasn't drunk-buying a house because I was reckless. I was doing it because, somewhere under the wobble, I knew I was done waiting.
- Laughter is one of life's best investments.
  You'll forget most of the sensible days, but you'll never forget the stories that make you laugh until you cry.

💭 Questions to Reflect On

If you're reading this and smiling, here are a few things to ponder, preferably with a pint in hand (water will do):

- When was the last time you did something spontaneous that turned out better than expected?
- Is there something you've been "thinking about" for years but haven't stepped toward yet? What's really stopping you?
- How often do you let yourself laugh at your missteps instead of judging them?

Chapter 5
Because Someone Said Yes

One decision can ripple farther than we ever imagine.

A year after recovering from brain surgery in 2007, I completed my fastest Ironman race yet.

I hadn't even been sure I'd ever race again. My surgeon wasn't convinced I would. Without the massive amounts of natural growth hormone that had once fueled my strength and endurance, I worried that the body I'd relied on, the one that carried me through long swims, endless miles, and stubborn hope, might simply disappear along with the tumour.

After the race, I wrote a report. Not just about race day, but about the year of loss, fear, rebuilding, and quiet resilience that led up to it. I shared my race report with friends and fellow triathletes.

At the time, I didn't know that my report would become part of something much larger.

Steve

A few years earlier, I had met Steve at the swimming pool.

I would arrive intensely focused on my swim training, probably a little too focused. Steve would often be floating in the deep end, gently bobbing up and down, always trying to strike up a conversation. At first, and I admit this with shame, I avoided him. My thoughts were something like: *I'm way too busy training to chat with some random guy.*

If I'm being honest, it wasn't just my training that kept me distant.

I was also quietly judging him.

Steve was a large man carrying extra weight, and without realizing it, I had already decided what that meant. I remember thinking, absurdly and unfairly, *Why doesn't he just move his arms and legs and burn off some of that excess weight?*

What makes that thought harder to admit is this: I'd been there myself. I'd carried extra weight. I knew how complicated bodies could be. And still, I judged him.

That judgment didn't come from cruelty. It came from habit. From my discipline-driven mindset. From a quiet belief I carried that effort always looks the same. Move more. Try harder. Push through.

Then one day, I wasn't swimming. I was deep-water running. I couldn't run on a solid surface due to yet another injury, so simulating running in the pool was my next best option. It's a pretty boring form of training, and conversation, any conversation, was suddenly welcome.

I finally *let* him talk. Mostly because I was out of breath.

And it turned out he was fascinating.

Steve was a retired paramedic. A musician. A songwriter and poet. He swam because it was the only thing that eased his generalized, crippling pain. Much of the weight I had judged was tied to severe liver disease. His body wasn't lacking motivation; it was surviving.

He needed a lifesaving liver transplant, and time was running out.

That realization landed hard.

I loved our conversations. Steve was genuine, warm, thoughtful, and deeply reflective. Facing the reality that his life might be shortened had sharpened his perspective in a powerful way. We became good friends.

In 2007, he became critically ill.

Reaching for Help

When Steve's condition worsened, I didn't know what else to do. How could we spread the word about organ donation?

I thought about the race report I had written years earlier. About the story that had quietly made its way beyond me.

And I reached out to the woman who had helped tell it.

Barbara's Story, Barbara's Voice

A friend named Emily, whom I met in a running club, had

once thought my Ironman story might resonate with others. Without telling me, she passed it along to a journalist at the *Toronto Star*, a remarkable woman named Barbara Turnbull.

Barbara had been paralyzed from the neck down since she was 18, after being shot during a robbery while working at a convenience store. Despite this, she became a respected journalist, raised millions for spinal cord research, and helped change accessibility laws across Canada.

As she interviewed me about my journey from brain surgery back to Ironman racing, we bonded deeply. Barbara understood adversity not as an abstract concept, but as a lived reality.

When I told her about Steve, and how desperately we needed more people to understand the power and ripple effects of organ donation, she didn't hesitate.

Within minutes, she replied:

"I need to do this story."

A week later, the *Toronto Star* published a piece about organ donation, hope, and lives hanging in the balance. Thousands of readers saw it. The number of people signing their donor cards rose dramatically.

A Country in Need of Donors

In Canada, organ donation rates remain heartbreakingly low. Even when people sign donor cards, the final decision often falls to grieving families in moments of shock and sorrow. Too often, the opportunity to save lives quietly slips away.

If you're able, please sign your donor card.

Talk to your family about your wishes.

Please say yes, if you can, to organ donation.

Not long after the article ran, a woman suffered a catastrophic illness and was not expected to survive. Her family was faced with an impossible decision amid overwhelming grief.

They knew what she had wanted.

They had seen Barbara's article; they chose generosity in the darkest moment imaginable.

That single decision saved five lives.

One of them was Steve.

The Ripples

Because of the courage of that donor's family, Steve went on to live many more years. Years filled with laughter, swimming, writing poetry, and deep time with his daughter and close friends. He even published a book of his poems, words that would never have existed without that gift.

A few years ago, sadly, Steve passed away due to other health complications. But without the donor, and without the family who said yes, he would never have had that time. Those memories. That legacy.

Barbara continued writing, advocating, and using her own story to champion accessibility and organ donation until her own premature passing at age 50. She did more with her life from a wheelchair, with her heart and voice, than many of us do on two strong legs.

And then there was the donor herself, whose final legacy was etched into five living bodies. Through the courage of her family, who honoured her wishes in their deepest grief, strangers were given the chance to keep living and loving.

Whenever I think of Steve, Barbara, the donor, and the family who made that choice, I am humbled.

Their courage, generosity, and determination remind me that sometimes miracles don't fall from the sky.

They happen because people are brave enough to create them.

Reflections

- Lives can be changed, and saved, through moments that feel almost incidental at the time.
- We so often confuse appearance with effort, stillness with laziness, and difference with deficiency, especially when it comes to human bodies.
- Legacy isn't only what we leave behind; it's what continues because of the choices we make.
- In their deepest grief, some people choose generosity, and the world is forever altered because of it.

Questions to Sit With Gently

- Have you ever judged someone quickly, only to later realize how much of their story was invisible?
- How do you feel about the idea that life and loss can coexist in acts of profound generosity?
- What kind of legacy do you hope your choices, large or small, might quietly leave behind?
- Is there a conversation you've been avoiding that could one day matter more than you know?

Chapter 6
The Ironman Catchers

There are no coincidences. Only meetings.
Elisabeth Kübler-Ross

Ironman wasn't something I ever planned on doing. In fact, for the first few years of my triathlon life, I placed "people who willingly sign up for a four-kilometre swim, 180-kilometre bike, and full marathon in one day" in the same category as people who enjoy kale smoothies or ice baths: suspicious at best.

And yet, after four years of sprint and Olympic-distance races, and four years of friends casually planting the seed that *you could totally do an Ironman* like they were offering me a slice of cake, I found myself saying yes.

Or rather, *they* said yes for me.

One warm July weekend in 2002, surrounded by three enthusiastic triathletes, Michael, Sergio, and Daryl, I somehow watched my hands type my name into the Ironman Lake Placid registration page while they hovered behind me like proud midwives.

"There! You're doing an Ironman!" they declared.

I gulped.

"What just happened?"

They beamed.

"You're welcome."

Just like that, my life shifted into a routine resembling a hamster training for the Olympics: sleep, eat, swim, bike, work, run, eat again, sleep. Repeat until victorious... or delirious. Whichever came first.

The Weird Symptoms No One Could Explain

Ironically, this was also the time my body began behaving as if it had secretly enrolled in a completely different endurance event. For someone supposedly in peak fitness, I spent an alarming amount of time at my doctor's office complaining about fatigue, joint pain, insatiable hunger, and, most embarrassing of all, lactation.

Yes. Lactation. The kind usually reserved for new mothers, not for women training for Ironman while needing to wear men's running shoes (another unexplained symptom).

In March 2003, my GP finally sent me to an endocrinologist, who dutifully ordered blood tests... but failed to notice that one result, growth hormone, was 17 times the normal range.

Seventeen.

Had that been caught, my life would have swerved in a completely different direction. Instead of gearing up for my first Ironman, I would've been wheeled into an operating room for brain surgery.

But fate, or serendipity, or divine triathlon intervention, had other plans. So, I accepted my new identity as a sweaty, hungry, leaking, exhausted medical anomaly and kept training.

Because once you're registered for an Ironman, there's no going back.

There's only going forward.

Race Week: Lake Placid

July 2003 arrived before I felt even remotely psychologically prepared.

Four of us piled into a car and drove seven hours, across the US border from Toronto to Lake Placid. This included my dear friend Fiona, a fellow Ironman first-timer, and two men we barely knew yet: Geoffrey, an IT professional, seasoned Ironman who looked like a Viking warrior and spoke calmly about Ironman as if it were a long walk. Jake was an engineer and project manager doing his first one... though "doing" might have been generous.

The air inside that car buzzed with nerves, excitement, and undeniable dread.

Fiona and I oscillated between *we've got this* and *what the hell have we done*?

Jake was honest. He'd been sick for months and had missed much of his training. His plan was to try to finish the swim. If he made it onto the bike, which he said was doubtful, he'd "see how far he got."

Fiona and I were appalled. Who comes all this way without believing they can finish?

We spent hours trying to encourage him, while privately doubting ourselves.

Fear, it turns out, is easier to manage when you're handing it out as encouragement.

The day before the race, we wandered through town and spotted a tiny church sign offering an *Ironman Athlete Blessing*.

Fiona grabbed my arm. "We need that."

I wasn't much of a churchgoer, as christenings, weddings, and funerals were as often as I'd set foot in the church, much to my mother's chagrin.

But Fiona was absolutely right. At that point, we needed all the help we could get: holy water, divine humour, guardian angels, whatever they were offering. That's where we met Friar Dan (more about him in the next chapter).

Sunday morning. 7 a.m.

A cannon fired, and 1,500 athletes sprinted, dove, and belly-flopped into the lake.

As a rookie, extremely excited and much too enthusiastic, I made the catastrophic decision to stand in the front row of athletes.

In hindsight: big mistake. Monumental mistake.

Within seconds, I was trapped in what can only be described as a full-contact, underwater spin cycle of a giant washing machine run by the devil himself.

I was elbowed, slapped, kicked, and at one point, someone *smacked my face* with an unidentified body part - possibly an elbow or a knee. Whatever it was, it hurt. My goggles were knocked off my face, and I gasped for air. I swallowed an unhealthy volume of lake water. While struggling to replace the goggles, someone hammered me across the back of the head.

I saw stars, then everything went black.

For a terrifying moment, I thought:

This is how I die? Six minutes into the race?

Not even dramatic. Not even a good story to tell.

Then I remembered the army of friends who'd travelled all this way to cheer for me and would be waiting at the finish line, as well as the charity donations people had pledged, and thought: Nope. Not today. Not like this.

I clawed my way to a rescue boat, gasping like a cat thrown into a bathtub.

A volunteer leaned over and asked if I wanted to get in.

"NO! If you touch me, I'm disqualified!" I sputtered.
(Translation: *I'd rather drown politely than quit.*)

I repeated my mantra:

Don't give up. Don't feel sorry for yourself. Enjoy.

Enjoy felt impossible, so I focused on the first two.

Somehow, through stubbornness, adrenaline, and maybe divine intervention from our visit to the church the day before, I restarted and finished the swim.

The Bike, the Run, and a Storm for Dramatic Effect

The 180-kilometre bike course was a roller coaster of relentless climbs. It seemed like the entire route slanted uphill in all directions. But, as it turned out, most of the uphills had a downhill, and every downhill made me believe I might, just might, survive the day.

The marathon that followed was a masterclass in human perseverance: the Ironman Shuffle. It came with torrential rain, sideways wind, and lightning that thankfully struck nowhere near me but added excellent dramatic ambience.

At one point, I even flirted mid-race with Jake, because apparently, Ironman turns me into a social butterfly with questionable priorities.

Despite the pain, weather, and intermittent existential crises, it somehow became the best day of my life.

The Finish Line and the Catchers

At 13 hours and 52 minutes, way faster than my 15-hour dream goal, I ran toward the finish line screaming with joy, arms flailing like an inflatable car-lot tube man.

Two volunteers were waiting for me, my catchers, because many finishers collapse at the end of the race. I didn't collapse, but I was bouncing, babbling, ecstatic, and borderline incoherent. They steadied me and asked how I felt.

I babbled something enthusiastic and unnecessary. They smiled kindly. They escorted me to the food tent for the well-earned cold pizza and cookies. Then to a desperately needed massage.

We were all pleasantly surprised that Jake made it to the finish line, deeply impressed by his determination to finish what he started. And somewhere in that mix of exhaustion and admiration... a little spark of interest began to grow.

We stayed in Lake Placid a few days after the race, wallowing in glory. When it was finally time to head back, the long drive home began. Halfway, around Kingston, we decided to stop for coffee and snacks at Tim Hortons. While waiting for my Timbits, I felt a tap on my shoulder.

"Excuse me... do you remember what you said at the finish line on Sunday?"

I turned to see a friendly man with warm eyes.

"I'm Doug," he said. "My wife, Irene, and I were your catchers."

For a split second, I wondered how on earth he recognized me. Then I looked down. It had been three days since the race, and I was proudly wearing every piece of Ironman gear I owned. Between the medal, jacket, cap, socks, and backpack, I was essentially an Ironman billboard.

"You said, *'I feel so good I could do it all over again!'*"

I nearly dropped my coffee. Apparently, my delirious rambling stuck with them, or at least helped. The whole race had inspired them so much that they decided to sign up for Ironman the next year.

Imagine that.

My exhaustion-fuelled nonsense became someone else's

inspiration.

I didn't know it then, but that strange, unstoppable energy, the endurance that made no sense, wasn't just grit or determination.

It turns out, a massive amount of circulating growth hormone can do remarkable things for stamina and drive.

I wouldn't recommend it as a training strategy; it comes with some serious, sometimes devastating health consequences, but at the time, it carried me farther than I ever thought possible.

The Full Circle

I thought that was the end of the story.

Life moved forward.

A week after the race, I emailed Jake.

Hi Jake. I hope you're doing well and recovering from the race. By the way, I fancy you, and I'd really like it if you took me out for dinner sometime.

Apparently, if I could finish an Ironman, I could do anything I put my mind to. It hadn't just strengthened my body; it had given me confidence in other parts of my life too.

We started dating soon after.

We raced Lake Placid again two years later.

Then, a few days after that race, we married on a dock on the lake at his parents' farm.

Five months after that, in December 2005, my health unravelled entirely. A shooting pain in my head sent me into brain surgery in early 2006.

The irony still makes me pause.

Had I been diagnosed in March 2003, I never would have done that first Ironman.

The event that shaped me so profoundly would never have happened.

Ten years after that first Ironman, on New Year's Day, 2013, while watching *The Princess Bride*, I remembered that one of the stars of that movie, André the Giant, also suffered from acromegaly. Curious, I searched the internet and learned that he had died from complications of the rare tumour I'd had. At the same age I was.

I felt a wave of gratitude.

Lucky to be alive.

Lucky for access to care.

Lucky for timing, even when it felt cruel.

Right then, I checked my email.

A message from a triathlete friend, Dave.

He'd just had coffee with a friend from his run group, a man from Wyevale (100 kilometres north of Toronto), who had been recently diagnosed with a rare brain tumour.

He was scared.

Could I call him?

His name was Doug.

Yes. **That** Doug.

My catcher from Lake Placid.

A decade earlier.

That same “rare” tumour.

My chest tightened as the realization landed. It felt like the universe had reached back through time, tapped me on the shoulder, and said: *Now it’s your turn*.

I called him immediately.

We met. I shared everything, the fear, the surgery, the long but successful road back, hoping it might steady him.

His surgery went beautifully.

His recovery was strong.

He and Irene returned to the joyful, active life they loved.

And that’s when I understood:

They caught me when I didn’t need it.

Years later, I was able to catch them when they did.

Life comes full circle in ways no one can plan.

🏃 Reflections

- Some things only become possible when we stop insisting on doing them alone.
- Help often arrives through people who owe us nothing, but who give anyway.
- There are seasons when strength means pushing forward, and others when it means letting yourself be held.
- Life moves like a relay: sometimes we run, sometimes we catch. Both roles matter.

💭 Questions to Take With You

- When has accepting help changed an outcome for you?
- What have you resisted because it required trusting others with your vulnerability?
- Who has carried you, emotionally or physically, when you couldn't do it yourself?
- In what area of your life might it be time to stop running solo?
- Where are you being asked to catch someone else now?

What Is an Ironman?

A friendly explanation for anyone wondering.

An Ironman is one of the toughest one-day endurance events in the world, consisting of:

🌊 3.8 km Swim

Open water. Hundreds of flailing limbs. Occasional facial assaults. Often described as "a washing machine with attitude."

🚴 180 km Bike

Hours of climbing, wind, nutrition math, and self-doubt.

🏃 42.2 km Run

A marathon completed on tired legs, shaky emotions, and pure stubbornness, usually in weather that seems offended you signed up.

🎉 Goal: Finish under 17 hours.

For perspective, while most of us are chasing the 17-hour cutoff, the pros now finish in nearly half that time. At the Ironman World Championship, Patrick Lange set the men's course record in Kona 2024 with an astonishing 7:35:53. On the women's side, Lucy Charles-Barclay stopped the clock at 8:24:31 in 2023. Same distance. Same island. Just an extraordinary expression of human endurance.

Canada's own Lisa Bentley, who raced while managing cystic fibrosis, once clocked 8:48. Just a very different pace of human possibility.

Despite its absurdity, Ironman has undeniable magic. It transforms people. Humbles them. Makes them cry, laugh, pray, hallucinate, swear, and, sometimes, flirt their way through.

And when the announcer calls your name...

"YOU are an Ironman!"

...it becomes one of the most unforgettable moments of your life.

Chapter 7
The Iron Friar

"Man plans, and God laughs."
Yiddish proverb

The day before my first Ironman in Lake Placid, Fiona and I spotted a sign outside a small church on the main street:

"Athletes' Blessing, All Welcome - 5 p.m."

It even had the Ironman logo.

We figured we needed all the help we could get, divine or otherwise, so that evening we went in.

Raised Catholic, I stopped going to church when I was 16.

But that day was different.

That day, I was desperate.

We stepped inside. Good news, I didn't get struck by lightning. So far, so holy.

The church was full of exceptionally fit, slightly nervous-looking people. Apparently, we weren't the only ones seeking intervention.

The service began with a christening: a crying baby, a splash of holy water, the whole deal.

Then the priest, actually a friar, invited all of the “athletes” to come to the altar.

I hesitated. First, I didn’t consider myself an athlete. Even after four years of training, that word still felt like it belonged to other people.

Second, standing front and center in a church as a lapsed Catholic felt like the perfect setup for divine retribution.

But Fiona nudged me, and up we went, along with about 15 others. Part of me wanted to laugh; a bigger part wanted to cry.

The friar smiled warmly.

“Welcome, everyone. I’m Friar Dan. I understand you’re doing the Ironman tomorrow. Wonderful! You must all love to swim?”

Some nodded. Some shook their heads.

All I could think about was the swim start the next morning: 1,500 athletes charging into the lake at once, fists, elbows, legs everywhere.

Friar Dan continued, “So that means you all love the water, right?”

He picked up the same bowl of holy water he’d just used for the christening...

...and suddenly, a wave of water splashed across 15 terrified triathletes.

We were soaked.

The congregation roared with laughter.

So did we.

Instantly, something loosened inside me: the fear, the tightness in my chest, the belief that I didn't belong in this "athlete" category. His humour did what logic couldn't: it reminded me I was allowed to be human.

He gave his blessing, wished us luck, and promised to see us at the start line.

As it turned out, he was known as **The Iron Friar**, a priest who completed the Lake Placid Ironman every year.

The race itself went well. There were elbows, fists, and even lightning that day; thankfully, none of the lightning hit me. I finished much faster than I had dared to dream.

In the years that followed, Lake Placid became familiar. I returned year after year for more races. Friar Dan would say grace at the athlete's dinner and then join us on the course, part priest, part steady presence.

In 2008, a couple of years after my brain surgery, my mum came all the way from England to cheer me on, her first time seeing an Ironman race in person. I told her about the Iron Friar, thinking she'd be impressed.

She was...

...though she also used it as ammunition.

"Paula," she said, "if Father Dan can do an Ironman, surely you can manage an hour in church once a week."

She and my Aunt Jan and Uncle Dave stood in the pouring rain on race day, cheering nonstop. I was soaked, exhausted, and happy to make her proud, even if I remained a disappointment in the churchgoing department.

A few days later, we drove the 700+ kilometres back across the US/Canada border to Toronto.

That next Sunday, Mum wanted to go to church.

At first, I couldn't even remember where the nearest Catholic church was, much to her horror.

Eventually, I recalled one: Joan of Arc, near High Park, about a ten-minute walk from home.

So, Sunday morning, Jake and I walked Mum there and left her to go to mass, while we went for coffee.

An hour later, we returned to wait outside.

The big church doors swung open.

Out walked Father Dan.

The Iron Friar.

He was even wearing his Ironman medal.

I stared, utterly confused.

"Father! What are you doing here? You're supposed to be in Lake Placid!"

He laughed. "Oh yes, my child. I'm the–"

But before he could finish, I blurted, "You're the Iron Friar! I raced with you in Lake Placid! But what are you doing here? This is Canada. It's a whole different country!"

At that moment, my mum came rushing out, eyes wide.

"Paula! It's the Iron Friar! If this isn't a sign, I don't know what is!"

Friar Dan smiled.

"I've just transferred here from New York State a few weeks ago. Welcome! This is your home now, too."

I muttered something about my fear of lightning... and right there on the street, he gently placed his hand on my head and blessed me.

I was mortified.

This was my neighbourhood.

What if someone saw me getting blessed in public?

Still, he smiled and said,

"There. All your sins are absolved."

If only it were always that easy.

It took a couple more miracles (stories for another time) and a few more years, but I now visit Joan of Arc on a semi-regular basis.

At some point, I stopped calling it coincidence.

Reflections

- Courage sometimes shows up disguised as humour, right when we need it most.
- Being truly seen by someone outside our usual world can change how we see ourselves.
- Permission doesn't always come from within; sometimes it's spoken into us first.
- Faith doesn't have to be loud or certain. Sometimes, it's just a quiet sense that we're not alone.

Questions to Sit With

- When have you found comfort or courage in an unexpected place or person?
- Is there a part of your identity you've earned but still hesitate to claim?
- Has someone ever reflected back a strength in you before you were ready to believe it yourself?
- What would it feel like to accept that you don't have to have everything figured out to move forward?
- Where in your life might reassurance arrive if you stopped insisting it look a certain way?

Chapter 8
No, I'm Not Transgender. I Just Have Big Feet

"Life is a tragedy when seen in close-up,
but a comedy in long-shot."
Charlie Chaplin

The guy I picked up during my first Ironman, Jake, eventually became my husband. The proposal, however, was not quite the romantic moment I'd always imagined.

Late in 2004, we'd been talking about marriage, and one day I said, "Maybe we should go ring shopping?"

The plan was to go on Friday after work. But on Thursday night, we had an argument (about what, I truly can't remember), and I didn't hear from Jake the next day. I panicked. I lamented to my work colleagues, convinced I'd ruined everything.

Then, finally, he called.

"How about dinner tonight?" he said casually.

Dinner? Not ring shopping? In my head, this could only mean one thing: he's going to end the relationship.

He arrived calm and friendly, which only made it worse. I'd already written the breakup speech *for* him in my head. We started cooking our favourite meal, salmon, sweet potatoes, and vegetables, when I blurted it out.

"Jake, are you going to dump me?"

He stopped mid-potato peel.

"What are you talking about, Paula?"

"Is this it? Are you dumping me?"

He stared at me, yam in one hand, peeler in the other, and said, "Paula, will you marry me?"

I blinked. "Is... is that a rhetorical question?"

He laughed, got down on one knee, and asked properly. Then he admitted he already had a ring, which explained why he didn't want to go shopping that night.

Not exactly the proposal I'd dreamed of.

Pre-Wedding Chaos

May 2005. We decided to keep things simple: a City Hall ceremony, just his parents as witnesses, followed by dinner. I wasn't a fan of church weddings, fancy dresses, or walking down an aisle with everyone staring at me. Plus, I hadn't been feeling great about my appearance or body lately... and honestly, I didn't even know what shoes I could wear.

The date was set for Saturday. I found a lovely periwinkle-blue suit with little flowers. It felt smart, simple, me.

Then, on Wednesday morning, just three days before the

wedding, disaster struck.

I was cycling to work in the bike lane when a car passed me and suddenly turned right. I had no time to stop. I slammed into the side of the car, flew forward, and somehow landed *on* the bike instead of off it. Pain shot from my crotch up to my chin, followed by a warm gush of blood.

The driver sped off.

Bleeding profusely through my shorts, I remembered my first aid training. Too embarrassed to call 911, I applied pressure to the wound by sitting back down on the bike seat. Then I pedalled very slowly and carefully for the remaining block and a half to my office. Heaven forbid I actually go to the emergency department. That would've been too logical.

I burst into the washroom, where my colleague Lucille was just leaving.

"Good morning, Paula, how are you?"

"Lucille!" I gasped. "I've had an accident. Get me some Betadine and gauze!"

Within minutes, half the office, my boss Annette, Maria, Stella, Jan, Tessa, Edna, and a few others, crowded into the washroom, insisting I go to the ER. Mortified, I finally relented.

At the hospital, I was ushered into a room and told to put my feet in the stirrups. The chief doctor came in, took one look, and exclaimed:

"Oh! Haven't seen one of these for a while."

Not reassuring.

He explained it was a straddling injury, common among

cyclists, though rarely discussed, and that I'd need quite a few stitches. A young female resident named Mimi came in to assist. She looked terrified. I couldn't blame her.

As the doctor worked, I tried to make conversation.

"So… when can I swim, bike, and run again? I've got an Ironman in two months."

He looked up. "Oh, you won't be doing any swimming, biking, or running for at least two or three weeks. You need to heal."

I gasped. "Oops! And my wedding's on Saturday!"

He chuckled. "You're more worried about the Ironman than your wedding?"

I explained my future husband was also an Ironman, and he would understand.

Out of the corner of my eye, I noticed Mimi slowly sliding down the wall.

She fainted.

The senior doctor didn't notice until I said, "Uh, you might want to check on your resident. She's on the floor."

He dropped his needle and thread. "Oh, crap."

He ran out of the room, leaving me in a very compromising position, my feet up in the stirrups. I leaned over the side rail of my gurney to comfort poor Mimi.

"You're going to be fine, just breathe. I'm so sorry! I knew it was bad, but I didn't think it was *that* bad."

Moments later, nurses rushed in with a gurney. Eventually,

they wheeled her out, and she was probably as embarrassed as me!

Only four people will ever see those 12 stitches: the doctor who stitched me, the resident who fainted, the gynecologist who checked me afterward, and my poor future husband, as I explained that we were *not* getting married on Saturday.

Reinventing the Wedding

Since I couldn't train for a while, Jake and I had some extra time on our hands. We thought about it and decided to plan a more "traditional" ceremony. Something meaningful. His parents had a farm with a picturesque lake, and we decided to get married on the dock we'd built together.

I had no intention of wearing a poofy, white wedding dress, but then, on a whim during a lunch break at work, I scribbled a little design on a scrap of paper: a sleeveless A-line with a floral bodice. It seemed simple enough.

Over the next few days, I visited every bridal shop in town, sweaty from cycling, clutching my soggy piece of paper. Most shopkeepers looked at me like I was an inconvenience wrapped in Lycra.

I felt my face burn beneath their tight smiles.

"Oh, custom design? That'll take at least six months and cost thousands," they'd say.

I was about to give up when I saw a sign in the final bridal shop:

Going Out of Business - Everything Must Go

Inside, a kind woman greeted me. I showed her my bedraggled drawing.

"I might have something just like this," she said. "I hope you're a size twelve."

I was.

When she brought out the dress, I burst into tears.

It was perfect. And it was only $250, a fraction of the other shops' prices.

Then came the shoes.

My feet had grown over the years, and nothing fit anymore. At that point, I didn't know why, though a podiatrist suggested it was caused by running and collapsed arches. He sold me expensive orthotics and suggested I start wearing men's shoes.

I went to Tallcrest, a specialty shoe store for larger sizes, where the man behind the counter gave me an immediate up-and-down look.

I picked up a shoe.

"That'll never fit you," he said flatly.

I tried another.

"Not even close."

"Can you please tell me what *will* fit?" I asked.

He sneered. "We don't have anything here for you."

I left the store in tears. Flashbacks from my childhood traumatic shoe-shopping experiences washed over me.

Married in My Bare Feet

A week later, on August 4th, 2005, we got married on the dock. I was barefoot. Everyone thought it was adorable. I played along, but inside I was crushed.

Five months after the wedding, I felt that sharp pain between my eyes, the one that changed everything. The tumour had been flooding my body with excess growth hormone. My feet hadn't just grown; *my whole body* had changed.

After surgery, I started to shrink. I lost 20 pounds quickly. My facial features softened, my skin thinned, and my men's running shoes started to slip right off.

So, I went back to Tallcrest for new shoes.

This time, the rude man wasn't there. A pleasant woman greeted me.

With much more confidence than the time before, I picked out a few pairs and brought them to the counter. She asked, "What size are you?"

I hesitated. "Honestly, I don't know anymore. I had a surgical procedure a few months ago, and my body's gone through some changes."

She smiled knowingly. "Ah, no need to explain, dear. **You're a transgender person!**"

I froze. "What? NO."

She panicked. "Oh! No! You totally look like a woman! I mean, you *are* a woman! I love your skirt!"

She backed into the stockroom as I shouted after her, "It was a brain tumour, actually!"

At first, I was devastated. I was only just starting to feel feminine and confident again, and now I was questioning *everything*, my body, my appearance, my feet, apparently.

But then it clicked.

I might not be laughing about this now, but this is absolutely going to become a story I can laugh at later.

A few minutes later, she reappeared with a tower of shoeboxes, eager to make amends.

I decided to have a little fun. Sitting up straight, pushing my chest out, smiling sweetly, I said:

"If I *had* had the surgery... do you think they did a good job?"

The poor woman looked utterly bewildered.

I laughed and told her it was an honest mistake, then shared the story about her rude colleague.

"Oh," she said knowingly. "That must have been Phillip. He has dyslexia and sometimes says the wrong thing."

I raised an eyebrow. "Dyslexia doesn't make a person unkind. And if that's his excuse... what's yours?"

She didn't even give me a discount that day.

Just to be clear: There's nothing wrong with being transgender. This was simply one of those moments when people make assumptions about feet, about bodies, about what someone "should" look like.

Reflections

- I thought I was reinventing my wedding. I didn't realize my body was already reinventing me.
- The moments that feel mortifying at the time often become the stories that we can laugh about later.
- Being misunderstood is uncomfortable, but it's also proof that we're human, and gloriously imperfect.
- Humour doesn't erase pain, but it gives us room to breathe inside it.

Questions to Smile With

- What's one moment from your life that felt like a disaster at the time but makes you laugh now?
- When plans unravel, do you tend toward panic, perfectionism, or humour?
- Have you ever been mistaken for something you're not, and what did that moment teach you?
- Where in your life are you still trying to fit into shoes that don't quite fit?
- What would it feel like to meet your most awkward, vulnerable self with a little more kindness, and maybe a grin?

Chapter 9
Honeymoon Disasters, Parts I & II

"The universe doesn't make mistakes.
It just makes things interesting."
Unknown

Our wedding was supposed to be a simple, sensible city hall affair. Something quick: "I do," a glass of bubbly, and a nice dinner. Somehow, we ended up having a reception with 170 people congregating in the back garden of my in-laws' farm, like a scene from a rural romance novel. Except this was real life, and real life comes with a bill. Which is why I decided we should save money on the honeymoon.

My brilliant idea?

Jake's fishing and hunting camp.

Just to clarify, I am *not* a hunting-and-fishing person. My idea of "rustic" is a hotel that stops room service at midnight. But Jake insisted the camp had been "recently rebuilt" and now came with "all the mod cons." Nestled in peaceful woodland, on the edge of a beautiful, calm lake with only two other cabins nearby, quiet, romantic, and free. The "free" part was extremely romantic to me.

There was, however, one tiny catch.

The cabin sat on Crown Land, and vehicles weren't allowed. So we parked 10 kilometres away and began our off-road honeymoon bike trek, Jake towing a trailer full of everything essential for a passion-fueled getaway: salmon, oysters, whipped cream, champagne, romance in perishables.

I love cycling, but off-roading? Not my forte. Jake zoomed ahead while I fishtailed all over the trail. Eventually, my chain fell off, and while I was wrestling with it, something bit my wrist. Hard.

A deer fly.

That sounds harmless enough.

But within minutes, a giant welt puffed up like rising dough.

Jake eventually circled back, asking why I was so slow. I showed him my swelling wrist. He nodded and, very casually, mentioned that he had just been charged by a bull moose, 1,500 pounds of antlered rage. But apparently *my* welt was the dramatic situation.

We kept going, because what else do newlyweds do in the wilderness? By the time we reached the cabin, I was itching everywhere. Under my arms, behind my knees, between my fingers, and in other areas that no one should ever itch on their honeymoon. The hives were spreading, my breathing getting tight.

That's when we discovered the downsides to a perfectly secluded honeymoon hideaway: absolutely no cell service. Or people. Or an EpiPen. I was, quite clearly, having a near-anaphylactic reaction in the middle of nowhere.

Luckily, I'd packed Benadryl. I swallowed a double dose... and passed out.

For two days.

So much for marital bliss.

When I finally woke up, puffy but alive, Jake was off fishing, apparently not overly concerned since I "looked peaceful." He assured me that he'd checked on me periodically, adjusting the blanket and reapplying insect repellent as required. In his defence, he was helping me in a practical/project managing/engineering way. As my eyes adjusted, I took in our surroundings. "All the mod cons" turned out to mean:

- no gas for the barbecue,
- an outhouse that wasn't working,
- and a fridge that had died dramatically in the August heatwave.

Our carefully curated honeymoon delicacies had transformed into a biohazard. How romantic!

So, we went fishing. I, who had fished exactly zero times, climbed into a rowboat, and we promptly started arguing about rowing technique, fish psychology, and whose fault the moose and the deer fly had been. Miraculously, we caught a 20-inch smallmouth bass. Jake cleaned it and cooked it over an open fire.

It was... edible.

Breakfast the next morning? Bass again.

At that point, I informed Jake that he owed me another honeymoon. Yes, the whole plan had been mine, but mutual suffering cancels all logic.

Honeymoon 2.0: The Earth Moved

In October 2006, we ventured to Kona, sun, ocean, and, for me, the holy land of Ironman. I pictured athletic inspiration and tropical bliss. We planned to volunteer and spectate at the Ironman World Championships (Ironman was definitely my passion/obsession). Jake came along out of love, resignation, or both.

We arrived at night and checked into our sixth-floor apartment. We could see only the silhouettes of the bay and a massive, glowing cruise ship. No food in the fridge, but we'd eaten on the plane. We were running a 10K race the next morning, so we figured we'd find breakfast before the race.

At 7 a.m., Jake left to pick up our race packets while I jogged down the main street, Ali'i Drive, in search of something, anything, to eat. It was Sunday. Everything was closed. But the ocean was pretty, the breeze warm, the morning peaceful...

...until I heard a rumbling sound. It grew louder.

My first thought was, "Subway train?"

Then I remembered I was in Hawaii.

Second thought: "Freight train? For... the main crops: macadamia nuts, coffee?"

Before I could invent a third theory, the entire ground began rolling like a giant wave. I dropped into a squat so I wouldn't fall. A woman nearby leapt out of her car, shouting, "What is happening to my vehicle? It's a rental! It's gone berserk!"

I tried to explain that it wasn't her car that was the problem, but I had no idea.

Then the sirens started blaring. I didn't realize immediately, but that was the tsunami warning system.

Another car stopped behind the frantic rental car lady. A man rolled down his window, completely unfazed, and shouted,

"It's an earthquake, lady!"

A 6.8 magnitude earthquake, as I later learned. I thought about my family and friends back home, hearing about a massive earthquake on the news that night. Was this the end? My next fleeting thought: people who know me won't be the slightest bit surprised that a disaster struck, with me in the middle, again!

Once the ground stopped impersonating a wave pool, I noticed, glancing down the road, that the crowd of runners waiting to start the race had started running uphill, away from the beach.

I sprinted back to the race start, where three local race organizers stood calmly watching the water as if they were supervising a BBQ. I babbled something like, "I'm on my honeymoon, the Earth moved, and my husband wasn't even with me!"

They laughed and told me to "chillax, lady," and explained that, yes, that was the biggest earthquake they'd felt in years, but that hill everyone had just run up was actually a volcano, and that sometimes when the "earth moves," the volcano gets angry. So, only if the ocean suddenly receded from the bay would that mean a tsunami. *Then* we'd run.

A true test of Jake's devotion: would he run for high ground or come back to meet me in our planned meeting place?

A few minutes later, he appeared, breathless, wide-eyed, and told me the apartment was trashed. Dishes everywhere, TV smashed, cupboards emptied by the earthquake's violent shaking. People had run onto their balconies in whatever state they'd been sleeping in... some of whom should definitely have stayed indoors or at least grabbed a towel to cover their nakedness.

Despite everything, the race directors shrugged and decided the show must go on. No electricity? Fine, they'd time it manually. Initially, Jake and I were excited that we might even win the race (only because we were the only two people at the start line), but then all of the other runners made their way down from the volcano. Our hopes of winning were dashed. The earthquake had shaken blossoms from the trees, carpeting the course in flowers. It looked like nature had decorated the road for us.

We ran. We survived. We took lots of photos. We finished, nearly last, but triumphant.

Only minor injuries were reported, though buildings cracked and roads split.

We enjoyed the remainder of our vacation, relatively uneventfully, other than the excitement of the World Championship Race, a thrill for me, so exciting to watch. I could only dream about competing there one day.

And that was Honeymoon 2.0.

Two honeymoons:

one anaphylactic nightmare,

one seismic event.

In hindsight, I'm not sure if the universe was sending warnings or simply testing my steadiness or my sense of humour.

Possibly all three.

Reflections

- Disasters don't always arrive as crises. Sometimes, they show up disguised as "romantic adventures."
- Survival isn't just about toughness; it's about flexibility, humour, and knowing when a situation is officially ridiculous.
- Foreshadowing is much easier to spot looking back. At the time, I chalked it all up to bad luck. Later, I learned that the universe will whisper, and if you don't listen, it will escalate. Sometimes from insects to moose to earthquakes.

Questions

- Have you ever stayed in a situation hoping it would "get better," even while ignoring early warning signs?
  What did you learn when you finally paid attention?
- When life shakes beneath your feet, literally or metaphorically, how do you tend to respond? Humour, panic, determination, denial? How well is that working for you now?
- When you reflect, were there any "moose charges" or "earthquakes" in your own life that you now recognize as early clues?
  What did those moments reveal about your needs, boundaries, or resilience?

Chapter 10
Miracles and Chocolate Creme Eggs

"There are only two ways to live your life.
One is as though nothing is a miracle.
The other is as though everything is a miracle."
Albert Einstein

January 2011

"I need to go back to England to look after my mother," I told my boss, fighting back tears.

He nodded with understanding. "Paula, do what you have to do. You need to take care of your mother."

I began preparing for the trip home, unsure how long I'd be there. The doctors said Mum likely had only a month or two to live, less if she developed an infection. Two years earlier, she'd been diagnosed with acute myeloid leukemia, discovered by chance when she tried to donate blood. After multiple rounds of chemotherapy and isolation, she became, at 69, the oldest person in Britain to receive a bone marrow transplant. Her donor was anonymous.

At first, it seemed the transplant had worked. She bounced back quickly, discharged after just 12 days. During her recovery, she returned to gardening, built a new fence and gate, rejoined the church choir, and took up mosaicking, creating intricate tabletops from broken glass and stone. But six months later, she collapsed. Suddenly, she couldn't walk, had lost her sight, and was disoriented. Doctors couldn't explain the confusion or blindness, but her bone marrow test brought devastating news: the leukemia was back. Further treatment would only prolong her suffering. It was time for palliative care.

I'd been a nurse for nearly 28 years, but nothing prepares you for caring for your own dying mother, a woman once so independent and proud, who now didn't even know my name.

Back Home

I returned to Durham, a small city in northeast England, where I spent most of my childhood. Mum had been discharged from the hospital a few weeks earlier. Her brother Joe had moved in to help, but none of us realized how much care she would need. She was crawling on her hands and knees from room to room, the safest way to move, since every time she stood, she fell, often hitting her head. It was heartbreaking to watch.

Even in her confusion and frailty, her determination was fierce. It might take her an hour to crawl up the stairs, and she sometimes fell asleep halfway, but she refused help. By the time she reached her bed, she was utterly exhausted.

Nights were the hardest. She'd wake gasping for air, and I'd lie awake listening, ready to help. I cooked flavourful, healthy meals, but she rarely ate. Once a week, she spent a day at the hospice, enjoying art therapy, Reiki, massage, and group support. A counsellor was offered to me to help navigate the pain and grief I was experiencing. Those Wednesdays were a small relief for both of us.

The Night I Thought I'd Lose Her

After a month, she developed a high fever. I urged her to go to the hospital, but she refused. Her blood pressure was dangerously low; her body was failing. My sister, Maria, came to help me as we bathed her and attempted to make her more comfortable. I dimmed the lights, put on her favourite DVD of an André Rieu concert, and sat by her bed, tears rolling down my face as she grew paler and weaker. When she began vomiting, I called the after-hours doctor, who diagnosed pneumonia. He recognized how distressing this was for me to watch, so persuaded my mum to go to the hospital "just for a short visit" and arranged an ambulance.

At the hospital, the emergency doctor took me into a small room where two cups of tea and a box of tissues were waiting. This was a typically English hospital way of preparing families for bad news. I'd sat with families in rooms like this. I'd been the nurse. The calm one. The explainer. The steady hands.

But now I was the daughter, and my insides felt so utterly empty and helpless.

"Your mother is gravely ill," he said gently. "She has septicemia and pneumonia. Her blood pressure is critically low; her heart could stop at any moment. I don't think antibiotics will make a difference. I'm sorry. You should prepare for the worst. She probably won't make it through the night."

Initially, I was numb.

Unable to reach my brother or sister (it was late, and they both have so many responsibilities with young children), I called Mum's friend, Clare, and asked her to contact Father Tony, our parish priest. He arrived around midnight and went in to pray with Mum and offer the Last Rites. I couldn't bring myself to stay in the room.

When he left 20 minutes later, I returned. She lay quietly, looking peaceful. I felt a surreal calm in the room.

"Did you have a nice visit with Father Tony?" I asked, not expecting much response.

"It was okay, Paula. He said some prayers," she said, clearly.

I froze. She knew my name. She hadn't recognized me in months.

Trying to steady myself, I asked, "Did Father Tony give you your Last Rites?"

"Yes," she whispered calmly.

As a nurse, I'd seen this before. We call it *the rise before the fall*, that sudden, almost miraculous lucidity after days or weeks of fading.

It's brief, and it's cruelly beautiful.

A final clearing. A last chance to say what matters – the words you didn't know how to say or were too afraid to say... until now.

What on earth can I say to make things better?

Then I remembered.

"Mum, do you remember when I was born two and a half months early, and the doctors said I wouldn't survive? They gave *me* the Last Rites, and look, I'm still here! And remember how, a few days later, they told you I might live but that I'd never grow above five feet (I'm almost six feet tall) and that I'd be *slow*?"

As I often do, I reached for humour, hoping it might lighten the mood.

Her response flabbergasted me.

"Well... at least they got one of those things right!"

"Mum... this might be our final conversation. Can we please be nice to each other?"

"Oh, Paula, I was only joking." She went from confused one minute to having her (dark) sense of humour back!

"Mum, just because Father Tony came tonight doesn't mean it's the end. You might be ready for this, but I'm not. Please hang in there."

She smiled, the first real smile I'd seen in months.

"Paula, I'm going to sleep."

I took a deep breath.

"*I love you, Mum.*"

Those words did not come easily. Saying it felt like stepping off a cliff. Not because I didn't mean it. I did. But because I'd spent a lifetime practicing not to.

My British, stiff-upper-lip upbringing had taught me: whatever you do, don't express your feelings. Even as she lay on her deathbed, the habit held me back. But I had to say it. And besides, I told myself, I probably wouldn't have to face her in the morning.

She didn't say it back, but I knew, in that moment and always, that she loved me too, even without the words.

She slept peacefully for the first time in weeks.

The Miracle

At dawn, sunlight filled the room. Mum opened her eyes.

"Mum, how are you feeling?"

"I'm hungry," she said.

Hungry? She hadn't wanted to eat in months!

"What would you like? There's yogurt, fruit, cereal..."

"I don't know. I don't fancy any of those."

Then I spotted a box of three Cadbury's Chocolate Creme Eggs on the bedside table.

"There's a chocolate Creme Egg here," I said.

Her face lit up. Though she couldn't see me, she turned toward my voice and almost growled, "Now you're talking!"

I could barely unwrap it fast enough before she devoured it.

"That was really good," she said, licking chocolate from her lips. "I feel a bit sick, but oh, that was good."

I didn't feel triumphant. I felt shaken. Because joy and grief were now living in the same room, and I didn't know which one to trust.

When the doctors came in moments later, they looked stunned. She was sitting up, alert, with chocolate all over her face. After examining her, one doctor frowned in disbelief.

"I can't really explain this," he said. "But your mum's pneumonia seems to have... resolved. It's gone."

The senior doctor took me aside. "She's still terribly unwell," he cautioned. "There's nothing more we can do for the leukemia. Let's transfer her to the hospice for end-of-life care."

A Return to Life

Two days later, she was admitted to the hospice, a beautiful place nestled in a ravine, with deer outside her window and sunsets over the trees. The care was compassionate and gentle. Each evening, the nurses brought around a trolley with tea, hot chocolate, wine, beer, and a selection of spirits, including Baileys Irish Cream. Mum's favourite was hot chocolate with a "healthy" splash of Baileys.

Nine days later, she was discharged *because she was doing too well*.

Who gets kicked out of a hospice?

Instead of attending her funeral, we took her to the seaside village where she had been the community nurse. She refused the wheelchair, linked my arm, and walked along the boardwalk.

From that day forward, she grew stronger. We went out for lunches, saw friends, and even attended an André Rieu concert. At one point, when Rieu spoke about "the healing power of music," I nearly shouted, "Hallelujah!"

Three months after I arrived, she walked with me to the local pub, The Duke of Wellington. We had a wonderful dinner and a great conversation, during which we discussed her wishes. I drank a little too much red wine, and even though she was still blind, she walked *me* home.

She didn't need me anymore.

After some planning, we got gadgets like a talking watch, a talking clock, and a talking kitchen scale. We also arranged for cleaners, window cleaners, and meal delivery. Day by day, she reclaimed her independence. Family and friends rallied.

Reluctantly, I returned to Toronto. I had to. My life was in Canada, and there were bills to pay.

A few days later, an email arrived from her hematologist:

> "Your mum is in remission. **There is no evidence of leukemia.** To have relapsed after transplant, to be so ill, and now look so fabulous, it's nothing short of a miracle."

Months later, doctors discovered the cause of her blindness: toxoplasmosis, a parasite likely caught from her neighbour's cat, Thomas, while she dug her garden after her bone marrow transplant almost a year before. Four eye surgeries later, her sight returned. In January 2013, she phoned me, laughing: "I've bought a car!"

With her permission, we had sold her car when she was blind and dying.

In May, she came to Toronto. Together we went to Las Vegas, flew over the Grand Canyon, and toured it by helicopter, a dream she'd always had.

In October 2014, we met in Paris, sipping coffee and eating croissants on a terrace on the Champs Élysées, climbing up the Arc de Triomphe, and watching the sunset from the Eiffel Tower.

The next year, we went to Rome, visited the Vatican, and had dinner with Father Tony, who was then serving there (and playing for the Vatican cricket team!). He would have tried to arrange an audience with the Pope, but the Pope was in Cuba during our visit. "Maybe next time," we laughed.

Today, Mum still lives independently in Durham, England. She drives, sings in the church choir, and volunteers at the hospice charity shop.

Every time I see a Cadbury Chocolate Creme Egg, I smile.

That winter was the most difficult time of my life, watching my mother shrink into confusion and weakness, when she'd once been the strongest person I knew.

And yet, somehow, it became one of the most amazing times of my life. Because it gave me something I didn't know we'd get again: moments of her. Moments of us. Moments that felt like borrowed time... and tasted like chocolate.

I didn't know then how much that borrowed time would teach me about surviving my own storms.

Years later, Mum told me she remembered that night, the prayers, the Last Rites, the quiet calm. When she was diagnosed with leukemia, she'd feared dying too soon, missing watching her grandchildren grow, never reaching her "golden years."

But in that moment, when she thought it was the end, she felt none of that. No fear. No sadness. Just a deep sense of peace and readiness.

She now calls it her "practice run." She says it taught her that the end, whenever it comes, isn't frightening after all, just calm.

I've held onto that ever since. It's comforting to know that what we fear most may not be what meets us.

Reflections

- Sometimes the moment we think is the end becomes the doorway to something we never expected.
- Even at our weakest, something in us remains fiercely alive; humour, will, love, spirit.
- Healing may arrive disguised as chocolate, music, or borrowed time.

Questions to Hold Gently

- Have you ever witnessed a moment that felt too small to matter, until it did?
- What has caring for someone you love taught you about presence, patience, or love?
- Where in your life might a small joy be doing more work than you realize?

Chapter 11
Esther: Life Is Strange, and Wonderful

Some of the most important turning points arrive disguised as ordinary kindness.
Anonymous

A Funny Thing Happened

In December 2015, I was laid off from my job as a diabetes nurse researcher.

That part wasn't funny.

But in hindsight, it was a long time coming. I'd been there 13 years, comfortable, surrounded by a wonderful team, and grateful for the Monday-to-Friday routine. The kind of job where you can plan a life... and occasionally remember what day it is.

Still, deep down, I knew I was ready for something else.

I love a challenge. I love helping people. Most of all, I want to feel like I'm making a difference. So, when the research funding dried up and I was let go, it turned out to be an unexpected blessing, just not the kind that arrives wrapped nicely with a bow.

What I *didn't* anticipate was how difficult it would be to find a new job.

In nearly 30 years of nursing, I had never been unemployed. Not once. Well, once, in the late '90s, for about an hour and then a job landed on my lap. Suddenly, I was entering a world I'd only ever heard about from other people, people with spreadsheets and résumés and the phrase "networking" in their vocabulary.

To make things even more fun, hospitals were laying off registered nurses and replacing them with care aides to cut costs. Patient care, of course, was what suffered most, but that's another story.

As they say, timing is everything.

Two weeks after my layoff, I had knee surgery to repair a torn meniscus. Maybe it was for the best that I wasn't working. I had plenty of time to recover and attend physio appointments... and develop an intimate relationship with ice packs.

By March, though, despite applying for countless jobs and completing courses to update my skills, I still had no leads.

None.

At this point, I was starting to feel like I'd been ghosted by the entire healthcare system.

Around the same time, worried about how I would pay the bills, I suggested to my husband that, after more than 12 years devoted to his PhD, he might consider exploring work outside academia.

Let's just say... that suggestion did not float into the room like a dove of peace.

It landed more like a bowling ball.

A Chance Encounter

At a follow-up appointment with my surgeon, I sat waiting on a bed in the fracture clinic when a nurse poked her head around the curtain.

"Hello! Your surgeon won't be long. It's a busy clinic. Thank you for your patience."

"No worries," I laughed. "I'm an unemployed bum; I don't have anything else on today!"

Then, without thinking (a theme in my life), I added, "Hey, by the way, I'm a registered nurse. Do you have any jobs here?"

She chuckled. "Oh! Are you serious? Not in this clinic... but let's go look on the intranet."

To my surprise, she ushered me to her workstation like this was the most normal thing in the world: *Come with me, random patient in a gown, let's get you employed.*

She helped me scroll through listings. I hadn't even considered this hospital before. It wasn't on my radar. But there they were: several full-time positions posted, right in front of us.

That nurse, whom I now know as Esther, went out of her way to help this "unemployed bum," and I'll never forget it. There was something so quietly generous about it. No fuss. No big speech. Just: *Here. Let's help you.*

I went home, applied for a role on the Cardiac and Vascular Surgery Unit, and a few weeks later, I had an interview.

It went well… except for the moment I made the entire panel cry.

It was *their* fault… They asked, "Who's your hero, and why?"

So, I told them about my mum and her battle with leukemia.

Oops.

Long story short: I got the job.

In June 2016, I started at St. Michael's Hospital. I'd never worked so hard or been so challenged physically, mentally, and emotionally, but I loved it. It was the kind of work that grabs you by the scrubs and says, *Welcome back to real nursing*.

I felt like myself again. Exhausted. But fulfilled.

An Unexpected Connection

There was a two-month gap between the interview and my start date, so I finally tackled something I'd been meaning to do: creating a support group for people with acromegaly and pituitary tumours, one I'd recovered from myself.

With encouragement from fellow advocates Deanna and Victoria, I started a Facebook group for people in Ontario and Central Canada.

Within weeks, we had 22 members, an impressive number, considering the condition affects only about three in a million people. I was basically running the most exclusive club in

Canada. Very VIP. Very niche. Not exactly the type of club you'd want to be in, but still.

During our conversations, we talked about treatments, specialists, and hospitals... and one woman, Esther, mentioned that her specialist was at St. Mike's.

"I just started working there!" I said. "Next time you're in for an appointment, we should grab a coffee. It's so rare to meet someone else with the same condition."

Her reply stopped me in my tracks:

"I work at St. Mike's too... in the fracture clinic."

The penny dropped.

Wait a minute... the fracture clinic?

It was her.

Esther was the nurse who had helped me find my job.

We both laughed in disbelief. Because what are the odds?

Life had come full circle in the most perfectly weird way. She had supported me when I needed it most, when I was scared and uncertain and trying not to panic about my future, and now, through this patient community, I was able to support her too.

We remain friends to this day.

Looking Back

Sometimes, the most unexpected moments shape us the most. Losing my job led me to a new purpose. A nurse's kindness created a lifelong friendship.

Life has a funny way of weaving everything together when we stay open, sometimes painfully, sometimes beautifully, but almost always with meaning.

And if there's one thing I've learned, it's this:

Serendipity isn't coincidence.

It's life's way of reminding us we're exactly where we need to be.

Reflections

- Not all turning points announce themselves as big moments; some arrive quietly, wearing scrubs and kindness.
- Purpose doesn't always come from ambition. Sometimes, it grows out of simply helping the person in front of us.
- Life has a way of looping back, not to impress us, but to remind us we were never as alone as we thought.

Questions to Sit With

- When has something that felt like an ending quietly turned into a beginning?
- Who has offered you help at a moment when you didn't yet know how much you needed it?
- What kind of impact do you have when you show up simply as yourself, without trying to fix or impress?
- Where in your life might meaning be unfolding gently, rather than dramatically?

Chapter 12
Is That All There Is?

Sometimes, life takes everything familiar
so you can discover what actually steadies you.

I had a great nursing position, a husband, and a full life racing in triathlons, and I was even faster now that I no longer had that pesky brain tumour. I was healthy. What could possibly go wrong?

The Condo with the View

We (I) decided to sell our townhouse, the one I'd bought impulsively after a few too many drinks (a surprisingly profitable decision in hindsight). I'd always admired a waterfront condo nearby. Many years earlier, a friend whom I used to run with would point it out, saying, "That's where all the rich and famous people live." I'm not sure that holds true, but it definitely piqued my interest.

One day, I noticed a unit that had been on the market for over a year, with the price dropping again and again. The online photos showed breathtaking views over Lake Ontario. I had to see it, even if just to peek into how "the other half" lived.

The moment I walked in, I was mesmerized. The condo itself was fine, but the view, oh, the view! I could see all the way across the lake to Niagara Falls, the Escarpment, the shimmering water. It was pure serenity. I fell in love instantly.

Trying not to make another "drunken townhouse" decision, I asked my agent to take me back. The second time, I still couldn't tear my eyes from the window. I knew this was where I wanted to be.

That night, I went home and told my husband, "Oops." Probably not the best opener. He wasn't thrilled; he was still immersed in his long academic track and comfortable in our current place. I'd been keen to move on for a few years. Honestly, if I'd waited for him to make his mind up, it probably wouldn't have happened. But eventually, he agreed. Our offer was accepted, and we moved in.

The condo, beautiful as it was, needed work, nothing urgent, but plenty of wear and tear. Still, I adored it. Every day, the lake view looked different, and I'd lose myself in its changing moods.

Ironman and Open-Heart Surgery

A few months later, I achieved something I'd never even dared to dream: competing in the Ironman World Championships in Kona, Hawaii. Me, a former couch potato, survivor, racing alongside the fastest triathletes in the world. Some of those athletes I'd only ever seen in magazines were now beside me on the start line. It felt surreal.

The race was both breathtaking and brutal. The Big Island was a furnace of ancient lava fields and volcanoes disguised as hills, long and unforgiving. The headwind on the Queen K highway felt like a giant hairdryer set to full blast, while sudden crosswinds shoved bikes sideways without warning. Every mile demanded respect. Every moment felt earned.

And still, it was extraordinary. Heat, wind, suffering, and deep gratitude. No earthquakes this time. Just Kona, in all its savage, unforgettable glory.

But while I was soaring, Jake faced his own battle. He needed heart surgery.

His recovery went reasonably well, but as he returned to his PhD studies, my patience began to fray. I'd been the main breadwinner for the duration of our marriage. It was wearing thin.

The Divorce

A year later, just after passing my three-month work probationary period and preparing for my first independent night shift, I checked the mail. A bank statement caught my eye. Our line of credit was carrying a balance I didn't recognize, large enough to make my stomach drop.

I've never been comfortable with debt. The only thing I've ever owed is my mortgage. When Jake came home, I asked him.

"Why is there so much on our line of credit?"

He hesitated. "Are you sure you want to talk about this now, Paula?"

"Yes. I do."

He started listing routine expenses. Tires. Brakes. Ordinary things.

I stared at him. “That doesn’t explain this amount.”

There was a long pause. Then he said, “I’ve retained a lawyer for our divorce.”

I went to work that night numb. We barely spoke after that. Counselling failed. Later, I understood he had been thinking about this long before I knew. I also recognized that I wasn’t blameless.

After nearly three years of legal battles, mediation, and endless paperwork, we settled. As part of the settlement, I lost almost half my pension and a significant portion of the condo, the home I had worked so hard for. Handing over that cheque broke my heart. I loved that view; it felt like steadiness, like somewhere I could finally exhale. But I didn't know how I could afford to keep the condo on my own. I would have to sell.

The marriage ending wasn’t the devastation. The long, slow unraveling had already done that. What hurt was the financial aftermath, the tangible proof of what it had cost.

Out of the Blue, a Glimmer of Hope

I met Helen in the condo gym, an outgoing, friendly woman who lived in my building. She approached me and asked if I was a basketball player, because she was recruiting for her team. I wasn’t, but we still became friends.

After a while, when she learned I might have to sell the condo, she offered to rent my spare room so I could afford to stay.

She said she'd been wanting to downsize and simplify her life, so it felt like a perfect solution for both of us.

It felt like a miracle.

Helen turned out to be the perfect roommate: clean, kind, and wonderfully organized. She reorganized my condo. Everything had its place. My home was spotless. I needed this. I'd always been a bit (actually, very) disorganized.

It truly felt like a new beginning. I felt as though I'd been climbing a steep, treacherous mountain for years, and now I'd finally reached the top. The view was spectacular.

Life was good.

For the first time in a long while, I let myself believe the ground had stopped shifting.

Everything Up in Flames

Then, one Saturday night while I was working a night shift at the hospital, the condo concierge called. "Your smoke detector's going off, but don't worry, we're checking it out."

False alarms were common, so I didn't panic. I was busy with my patients, so I didn't think about the call. But when no one answered my calls an hour later, I knew something was wrong.

Helen finally called, her voice shaking: "Paula, you have to come home. I just got home... the condo... it's destroyed."

By the time I arrived, fire trucks lined the driveway. Several inches of water pooled on the floors. Furniture was blackened beyond recognition. Almost everything I owned was gone.

Blackened. Ruined. But the pit in my stomach was darker still. What terrible thing in my life (or previous life) had I done to deserve this?

As if that wasn't enough, the next day, I had to fly to England for my uncle's funeral. The suitcase I'd packed before leaving for work the night of the fire still reeked of smoke. I hadn't told my mum about the fire, as she was grieving the loss of her brother. My insurance adjuster reassured me that everything would be taken care of, and I should go back to England. When my mother hugged me upon my arrival, she sniffed my clothes. "Paula, have you started smoking?"

I laughed through tears. "No, Mum, my condo burned down yesterday."

She took me home, poured me a glass of Baileys, and played Peggy Lee's song *Is That All There Is?,* the one where she sings about her childhood home burning down and wondering, "Is that all there is to a fire?" Mum, as she usually did, said all the right things to comfort me and made me laugh through the grief.

It's strange how laughter works, even in the darkest moments. Sometimes, just sharing a laugh can help you exhale and feel lighter, if only for a moment. When you're in pain, those tiny sparks of joy, like a song, a joke, or a memory, can bring a bit of relief, even if the world is still smouldering around you.

The Spark of Hope

Investigators later found that the fire started from the box of batteries stored loosely in my perfectly organized pantry. A spark ignited. My insurance company denied most of my claim, saying I'd signed a clause that excluded certain coverage. I felt like I'd lost everything twice over, through divorce and now through fire.

Back home in Toronto, at my lowest, on a bitterly cold night, probably minus twenty degrees Celsius, I went for a walk with my camera and a bag of birdseed. I was exhausted from losing. It felt like every time I stood back up, something else knocked me down. I didn't know how much more I had in me. Desperate for even the smallest inkling of hope, I watched swans, ducks, and geese glide across the icy water.

As I fumbled with the camera settings, my fingers numb with cold, I glanced over the lake and saw a huge orange moon rising over the city. Almost as bright as the sun, it felt like an impossible glow, a quiet promise in the dark.

It took my breath away.

For the first time in months, I felt hope.

Later that evening, a kind neighbour, Robin, reached out. He was a retired insurance professional and asked to review my policy. Hours later, he emailed back:

"Paula, you're entitled to everything you've claimed. They're not being honest with you."

He gave me the contact for the insurance ombudsman. I wrote that night. The next day, my adjuster magically "discovered" that I did, in fact, have the $150,000 in coverage she'd told me I didn't.

I was furious, but also relieved. Eventually, my condo was rebuilt. A new kitchen, new floors, new furniture, appliances, and everything that really needed upgrading was replaced, and I was able to breathe again.

I realized then that life can take everything from you, your health, your marriage, your home, but if you can still see the beauty in a moonrise or sunrise or anything, you haven't lost it all.

Maybe that's what Peggy Lee was really asking in her song:

"Is that all there is? If that's all there is, my friends, then let's keep dancing."

Reflections

- Loss can strip away everything except who you are, and that's where rebuilding begins.
- Hope doesn't mean that everything is OK in the moment, but it gives us the space to create the possibility that things will get better.
- Serenity isn't something you own; it's something you carry. The view mattered. The condo mattered. Peace returned the moment I let myself be moved by something as simple as a moonrise.
- We don't get through devastation alone. Hope arrived through other people, a roommate, a neighbour, my mum with Baileys, and Peggy Lee. Resilience is rarely a solo act.

A Few Questions to Sit With

(You don't need answers. Just honesty.)

- When has something you thought would destroy you quietly reshaped your life instead?
- Where do you currently look for peace, and what would it mean to find more of it within yourself?
- Who has shown up for you when you didn't know how to keep going?
- What small moment of beauty has helped you breathe again during a hard season?

🔋 One Unpoetic, Practical Thing I Learned

Loose batteries can spark and cause fires. Store them safely, ideally in their original packaging or a proper container, with terminals covered and away from anything flammable.

It's a detail you don't think about until the unthinkable happens.

I think about it now.

Chapter 13
The Empaths' Curse (or Blessing) and Being in the Right Place at the Right Time

---

"We are all just walking each other home."
Ram Dass

For most of my life, people have appeared exactly when I needed them.

Helen.

Robin.

Friends, colleagues, neighbours, strangers who stepped in without asking for anything in return.

Only later did I realize that, just as often, I was being placed on the other side of that exchange.

Those seasons showed me both sides of the equation: what it feels like to be the one who is rescued... and what it means to be the one who shows up.

Just as often as I've needed saving, life has dropped me into situations where I was the one holding the metaphorical (and sometimes literal) gauze, oxygen mask, or emotional duct tape.

Fires, floods, freak accidents, you name it: if there's chaos, there's a decent chance I've stumbled right into the middle of it.

Which brings me to another thread that's been quietly running through my whole life: the strange, exhausting, beautiful reality of being an empath, and of ending up, over and over again, in exactly the right (or wrong) place at exactly the right time.

Catching What My Patients Have

There's something about being an empathetic person. I'm not sure whether that's what drew me to nursing, or whether nursing somehow drew *me* in. But it's fair to say that every time I've worked in a particular specialty, I've mysteriously managed to develop the very condition I was caring for.

Almost every time. I never did get pregnant while working on the maternity ward, thank goodness.

My first experience with this strange phenomenon began on the trauma orthopedic ward at Mayday Hospital, just south of London, England.

Around that time, my friends Helen, Joanne, Jill, and I booked what sounded like an irresistible skiing holiday in Bulgaria. Two weeks, all-inclusive: flight, food, alcohol, ski rental, and accommodation, for the grand total of $350.

How could we refuse?

When we arrived, we were told there hadn't been snow for

three weeks.

“Not to worry,” said our overly enthusiastic host, “the mountain range still has snow. It’s just a little *crispy*.”

Another word for crispy, we soon discovered, was icy.

So there we were, at the top of a mountain, kitted out with shiny new gear, staring down the steepest of all runs: a double black diamond. The beginner “green and blue” slopes were closed due to poor conditions, and, truth be told, we were novices in every possible sense. Our skiing experience consisted of two awkward lessons on artificial slopes that felt more like oversized hairbrush bristles than snow.

The only way down was to throw caution (and perhaps common sense) to the wind.

It took us six hours to descend, mostly on our backsides, skis in hand, alternating between laughter and panic. By some miracle, we survived.

But my survival came with a few souvenirs from that two-week getaway: a snapped ski, a concussion from colliding with a boulder, a dislocated shoulder, and a fractured thumb.

Luckily, I worked on a trauma orthopedic ward.

When I returned home, I was patched up like a professional, but even I could see the irony.

It felt like a sign to move on.

After that, the pattern became harder to ignore.

General surgery and geriatrics were followed by a hospital admission of my own, diverticulitis, a condition usually reserved for people three times my age. Thoracic respirology brought exercise-induced asthma, latent TB, and a lung nodule scare. Diabetes research delivered diabetes. Cardiac and vascular surgery gifted me varicose veins, courtesy of a knee surgery gone wrong. Each move came with a diagnosis, each diagnosis with the same quiet question: coincidence... or curriculum?

At some point, I stopped being surprised and started being curious. Randomness felt harder to live with than meaning. I started to think that maybe I should be very careful about which specialty I choose next. Palliative care crossed my mind, but given my track record, friends and colleagues strongly advised against it.

Day Surgery... and the One-Woman Clinical Trial

Onward to the Day Surgery Unit.

A safer choice, right?

Apparently not.

In five years, I became a frequent flyer: a breast lumpectomy, a total hip replacement, a total knee replacement, and another (yes, again) "straddling" injury.

At this point, I'm half convinced I was running a one-woman clinical trial.

But here's the thing: it wasn't just happening in hospitals.

It was everywhere I went.

The Man in the Lobby

One evening, while talking with Aimee, who worked at the concierge desk, a man staggered into the lobby, blood streaming down his face. He looked like he'd been attacked with a machete, a gaping wound across his skull, yet he calmly pressed the elevator button as if nothing was wrong.

Instinct took over. While Aimee called 911, I grabbed his jacket and pressed it to his head, applying pressure and trying to convince him to sit before he collapsed. In those frantic moments, my mind raced with thoughts like, "Not again!" and I worried the man with the machete might still be nearby.

He resisted, so I pretty much had to wrestle with him to keep him from getting into the elevator. His words were slurred as we asked for his name.

By the time paramedics arrived, I'd wrapped his head as best I could.

His partner arrived as he was loaded into the ambulance. She explained he had leukemia and low platelets, which caused the bleeding, and that his slurred speech was from chemotherapy. I worried he might not survive.

As it turned out, he hadn't been attacked with a machete. He'd tripped and fallen, headfirst, behind the condo.

A couple of months later, at our condo Christmas party, he spotted me from across the room, ran over, and gave me the biggest hug.

He'd recovered.

And he remembered.

That hug made all the chaos worth it.

The E-Bike Artery and the Almost-Wedding Invite

It's happened over and over again.

Last summer, biking home from work, I noticed a man on the ground, his leg in the air, blood everywhere. He'd severed an artery in a freak accident with an e-bike.

He was terrified and asked, "Am I going to die?"

I said everything I could to reassure him.

In my head, I knew the truth: with a severed artery, he could.

His cousin and I pressed so hard on the wound that our hands cramped. I made a temporary tourniquet using his t-shirt. Slowly, the bleeding began to ease. We held steady until help arrived.

In the end, he kept apologizing, embarrassed for "causing so much trouble."

I shared a suitably personal emergency story of my own, the time I fell onto my bicycle and needed stitches in a very private body part, and one of the doctors fainted.

That got him laughing, probably the last thing you expect when you're convinced you're about to meet your maker.

He invited me to his cousin's wedding the next day.

(I declined, but it was sweet.)

He made it through emergency surgery, and surprisingly, he

attended the wedding that weekend.

Emergencies at 30,000 Feet

It's not just on the ground.

I've resuscitated strangers on streets and assisted on flights. Once, mid-flight, a baby lost a toe due to a freak incident with the change table in the washroom. Another time, a woman had a massive seizure during a flight that no one else noticed.

From "Why Me?" to "For Me"

For a long time, I used to ask:

Why me?

Why do these things keep happening to me?

I've started to see it differently.

Maybe they're not happening **to** me.

Maybe they're happening **for** me.

Because each experience, every illness, every accident, every moment when someone needed help, has shaped me into the person I am.

And perhaps that's why I'm here:

to help, to heal, to comfort, to inspire.

Ultimately, this is why I'm sharing my stories.

So perhaps empathy is a superpower, though I'll admit it's

come with its fair share of bumps, bruises, and biopsy results.

Still, if being an empath means attracting a bit of chaos along the way, I'll take it.

Just as people have appeared exactly when I needed them, I've learned to appear for others, with steady hands, an open heart, and whatever version of gauze the moment requires.

Maybe we really are just walking each other home.

Reflections

- Empathy is both a gift and a magnet. It draws people - and moments - that need care.
- Life's curriculum isn't always gentle. Sometimes the lesson arrives as mayhem.
- Humour is medicine too. Not denial. Survival.
- Purpose shows up in hindsight. One day, the dots connect.

Questions to ponder

- Have you noticed a repeating pattern in your life that kept showing up until you learned something?
- When have you been called to help, unexpectedly, inconveniently, but unmistakably?
- How do you care deeply without losing yourself in other people's pain?
- Can you think of something that happened *for* you rather than *to* you?
- If your life is a tapestry, what threads keep appearing: empathy, humour, hope, purpose?

Chapter 14
The Trip That Saved Me

Detours don't announce themselves as blessings.
They arrive as interruptions.

How many times can one woman hit the snooze button? Apparently, infinitely. I really should just have gotten up the first time the alarm went off, but here we are again, with me launching into my trademark morning mayhem like a chicken with its head cut off.

"Shit, shit, shit, I'm late!"

I fell out of bed, stumbled to the loo, and skidded into the kitchen. Thankfully, I loaded the coffee pot the night before. Small mercies. Quick shower. Nearly wiped out on the tile. Saved myself with the grace of a drunken flamingo.

Back to the kitchen. Made my smoothie. Accidentally tipped an entire bag of chia seeds across the counter... and the floor... and the walls. Anyone who has ever dealt with chia knows it's basically glitter with a superiority complex.

Thank God for my DustBuster.

Lunch packed. Coffee mug filled. Out the door.

The Fall

I pressed the elevator button... and suddenly, it felt like everyone in my condo had decided to take the elevator at the exact same moment. I waited. Thirty seconds passed. I don't *have* thirty seconds. If I'm not on that elevator instantly, I miss the bus.

And sure enough, I missed the bus. I saw it pulling away like it was personal.

Fine. My backup plan was to run to the next stop. (I knew a shortcut.)

It was dark and raining, and I was wearing brand-new running shoes with thick cushioning, which felt like they altered the laws of physics. I was sprinting, which I absolutely shouldn't have been doing, and I could see the bus. It was still there, but the doors were closing. I was 20 feet away when my foot misjudged the curb, thick sole meeting low curb, and I went fully airborne.

Snap.

Something in the back of my leg snapped. Pain and a strange sensation of warmth rushed down the back of my leg. Then the rest of me went face-first into the pavement.

I do not have time for this.

Somehow, I dragged myself and my traitorous leg to the bus, pounding on the door as the driver pulled away. He reluctantly opened it. Great. This is the same driver I see every morning, and today I'm bleeding down my face like an extra in a zombie movie.

He asked for my bus pass.

I said, "No pass. You know me. I need to sit."

He squinted. "Paula, you're looking rosy this morning!"

"That's not rose. That's blood."

He still wouldn't drive until I showed the pass, so I flashed it and collapsed into a seat. The rest of the ride is a blur.

At our stop downtown, he suddenly sprinted off the bus and into the nearby coffee shop. He returned with a cup of ice, handing it to me like it was the Holy Grail. I appreciated the gesture, but had no idea what to do with a single cup of ice when half my leg seemed to be hanging off.

The Misdiagnosis

I don't remember exactly how I made it to the hospital, my own workplace, but somehow, I did. I do recall people staring at the blood pouring down my face. Not one person asked if I was okay.

Because... society.

While waiting in the emergency department, I called my manager.

"Hi... It's me. I'm going to be late. Again. Another accident."

She barely paused. At this point, calamity had become part of my brand.

A doctor assessed me and asked me to lift my leg. I could, using compensation and stubbornness, skills I'd perfected over years of sport. He nodded, unconcerned.

"Strain," he said. Ice. Ibuprofen. Rest.

I went home. I waited. I tried to believe him.

But the pain didn't improve. It deepened. An impressive bruise bloomed, purple and black, stretching from my bum to my ankle. That wasn't a strain. That was modern art.

A sports medicine doctor ordered an ultrasound. It showed a rupture. An MRI was needed to be sure.

Eight weeks later, the MRI confirmed it: all three hamstring muscles were completely torn.

By the time I saw the surgeon, his face told me everything before he spoke.

"You should have had surgery immediately," he said. "Now it's too late. The muscles have atrophied. Surgery would likely do more harm than good."

He paused.

"Paula... your triathlon days are over."

I'd heard versions of that sentence before.

This time, it felt real.

No hamstring: no running, no riding, no power walking.

I got second and third opinions.

Same answer.

So, I do what any devastated athlete would do: I bury myself on the couch and eat bonbons like it's an Olympic sport.

For two months.

The Mirror and the Mammogram

Then one morning, I snapped out of it. Again, I decided that this cannot be my life.

After all, the doctors have been wrong before.

I weighed myself and saw I'd gained 20 pounds. Time for drastic action. I cleaned up my eating habits, got moving, and started walking, biking, and swimming. I wasn't as strong or as fast as before, but I can move, and I'm sure I can improve. Slowly, the weight came off.

A few weeks later, standing in my bathroom one morning, I caught something in the mirror. A slight crease. An asymmetry under my right breast. Nothing dramatic, just... off.

I shrugged it off initially, blaming weight fluctuations and age changes.

But then I remembered: my brain tumour diagnosis years earlier had put me at a much higher risk for breast cancer.

Coincidentally, I had a mammogram scheduled for next week. I mentioned my concern to the technician performing the test. She took my concerns seriously, and, in addition to the mammogram, she did a particularly thorough ultrasound and sent me home.

The next day, my doctor called.

"Paula, you need a biopsy at Princess Margaret Hospital (the cancer hospital) tomorrow. Everything is shutting down because of COVID, but you need to go."

That's when I knew it was serious.

I got the biopsy. A week later, the diagnosis: **breast cancer.**

The good news: not aggressive.

The bad news: surgery and radiation will be delayed indefinitely because of the pandemic.

Cancer in a Pandemic

Diagnosed with breast cancer the day the COVID pandemic started.

Just my luck.

Of course, I still had to work. I was often redeployed to the emergency department, terrified that getting COVID would delay or cancel my surgery altogether. PPE was limited. The ER was the last place I wanted to be. At that point, none of us really understood how the virus spread, and even less whether our protective equipment was actually protecting us.

Because I'm an open book, I posted on social media:

"Next chapter: I have breast cancer."

The response was overwhelming. Friends, neighbours, coworkers, even people I hardly knew, showed up with messages, meals, flowers, and kindness. At work, colleagues gathered in full PPE and offered what passed for group hugs, arms hovering awkwardly in midair. Those gestures meant the world to me.

Enter Patrick

Around this time, I went on a blind date with a guy named

Patrick. Tall, gentle, handsome, a little quirky, but interesting. On our first COVID-safe, six-feet-apart walk, he asked if we could meet again. We had a lot in common: photography, cycling, paddling.

I said yes, but told him the truth.

"I've just been diagnosed with breast cancer. I have no idea what the next few months will look like. You can run for the hills if you want."

He paused, thought for a moment, then said, "Oh, Paula... I'm not really a boob guy."

I nearly fell over laughing.

And that was that. We kept meeting. Walking. Talking. Six feet apart. For months.

That Proclaimers song could have been our theme:

I would walk 500 miles... a pandemic version, six feet apart.

At home, Helen was spiraling. Or at least, that's how it looked to me. I assumed her OCD fears had kicked into overdrive. She became hyper-vigilant, convinced I'd bring the plague through the front door. Conversations shortened. Doors closed. The house grew tense in a way I couldn't quite name at the time.

It became uncomfortably strained.

Thankfully, I didn't have to wait until the pandemic was over for surgery. I was given a date a month later. Patrick came to every appointment, waiting outside Princess Margaret Hospital each time. On surgery day, he handed me a story he'd written the night before about a dragon who finds a lump under her wing. It was ridiculous, hilarious, and full of inside jokes. I read it between pre-op tests and was wheeled into the operating room laughing.

The staff probably thought I was unhinged.

(In hindsight, I probably was. Just a little.)

I recovered well physically.

Emotionally, things at home got worse.

Helen, Fear, and the Boiling Point

Helen barely spoke to me. I felt like a stranger in my own home. Honestly, I half expected to come back one day to a rabbit boiling on the stove.

Eventually, I confronted her, gently.

Two days later, she gave notice.

We barely spoke after that.

I wasn't sad when she left.

During radiation, Patrick travelled with me to all 20 sessions. Sometimes we cycled the 10 kilometres to the hospital. Sometimes we took the bus when I was too tired to ride. My community kept showing up with quiet, steady kindness.

I felt carried through that season.

Almost euphoric.

Patrick and Parting Ways

Patrick and I dated for a while longer, but eventually we realized our personalities and lifestyles didn't quite mesh.

We remain friends. And I will always remember, deeply and gratefully, how he supported me through one of the most stressful and frightening periods of my life.

Some people enter your world for a season, some for a purpose.

Patrick's purpose was meaningful: he held me up when I needed it most.

Helen's Call and the Final Twist

By then, I thought the strangest chapters of that year were behind me.

Six months slipped by. On New Year's Day, Helen called. I was surprised. I hadn't heard from her since she moved out.

"Do you know what happened to us?" she asked.

"No," I said honestly. "One day, we were friends and getting along well." (I almost said *like a house on fire* but thought better of it.) "And the next, you went cold."

"Paula," she said quietly, "I fell in love with you."

Well.

That explained everything.

Life, once again, had its own script, bizarre, unexpected, occasionally hilarious, and always serving up the lesson I didn't know I needed.

And all of it, the hamstring, the fall, the rupture that ruined my stride, led me to the mammogram and particularly careful ultrasound that caught my cancer early.

A trip, literally, that saved my life.

Reflections

- Even detours can become lifelines.
  If it hadn't been for the hamstring rupture, I wouldn't have slowed down enough to notice the changes in my body.
- Community is often the medicine we don't know we need. Asking for help isn't a weakness; it's wisdom.
- Hard seasons reveal who truly belongs in your life. Crisis has a way of shaking loose what's no longer aligned, homes, relationships, identities, and bringing in the people who genuinely see you, support you, and love you, not just your circumstances.

Questions

- When life has thrown you off your planned path, did something unexpected, maybe even unwanted, ultimately guide you somewhere important?
- Who in your life shows up for you when things fall apart, not just when they're going well? And do you let yourself lean on them?
- What situations or relationships in your life feel "heavy" or misaligned, and what would it look like to gently release them in favour of lighter, more authentic living?

Chapter 15
When the Lights Came On

"Be curious, not judgmental."
Walt Whitman

No matter where I went, the wiring came with me: missed buses, spectacular wipeouts, impulsive decisions, broken bones, and a brain permanently set to fast-forward.

For years, I'd written it off as bad luck, clumsiness, or just "Paula being Paula."

But as I limped into yet another recovery, another knee surgery, and was finally forced to sit still, a small, uncomfortable thought crept in:

What if there was a pattern here?

What if none of it was random?

It was as if someone had finally switched on the lights in a house I'd been stumbling around in for decades, bumping into furniture, tripping over rugs, apologizing to guests for the mess, and assuming all of it was entirely my fault. But once those lights flickered on, every odd detail of my life, every chaotic detour, every impulsive, clumsy, hilarious misadventure snapped into sharp focus.

Oh.

This wasn't just *me being me*.

My brain had probably been doing acrobatics since the day I was born.

Why did nobody tell me?

Maybe people suspected. Were they trying to be polite? Or perhaps they assumed I'd figured it out on my own. It took knee surgery, yet another unplanned "pause" in my endless carousel of activity, to finally force me to sit still long enough to truly think.

And that's when it happened.

Scrolling through an article one quiet afternoon, I began reading about **ADHD** in adults... and suddenly felt as if I had discovered the missing chapter of my entire life.

Every sentence, every symptom, every description had me nodding like one of those dashboard bobbleheads.

My past wasn't random. It wasn't bad luck or clumsiness or chaos for chaos's sake. It was a pattern, elegant, complicated, sometimes inconvenient, hiding in plain sight for 58 years.

The School Years: Foreshadowing Nobody Noticed

Let's start with the infamous school reports. The ones written in tight, judgmental cursive that always began with promise and descended into confusion.

"She's bright but easily distracted."

"Needs to concentrate."

"Talks too much."

"Silly attitude."

"Cannot control herself."

"Cannot control herself" felt slightly dramatic. I wasn't setting fires.

I wasn't particularly hyperactive, but my mind was always on overdrive.

While my classmates sat cross-legged on the carpet during story time, I sat perfectly still, replaying the story ahead of the teacher, rewriting the ending, and wondering what would happen next. My body stayed put. My thoughts did not.

But back then, it wasn't "attention deficit hyperactivity disorder."

It was "needs to try harder."

Nobody suspected my brain was wired differently. They just saw a girl sitting still while her thoughts ran marathons.

A Lifetime of Bumps, Bruises, and Broken Bones

Fast-forward several decades, and let's discuss my ongoing feud with gravity. I've broken 27 bones. Yes, you read that correctly. Twenty-seven.

There were the skiing accidents, the bike accidents (plural), the time I fell off a chair while sitting "still," and the memorable day I tripped over absolutely nothing in a parking lot and sprained both ankles at once. At this point, the emergency room should have handed me a loyalty card. Every seventh visit, free coffee!

In hindsight, it wasn't just clumsiness.

It was distraction. Impulsivity. A brain that moves faster than physics.

When your mind is already on Step Four, your body tends to collide with Step One.

The Impulsive Decisions

And then there were my spontaneous life choices, the ones that seemed like spectacular ideas in the moment. Like the time I bought a townhouse after a St. Patrick's Day race and a few celebratory green beers. Most people browse. Compare. Budget. I sign on dotted lines while still wearing sweaty running clothes.

Looking back, I realize it wasn't recklessness.

It was enthusiasm in its purest form.

My impulsivity wasn't a flaw; it was the engine driving my life forward.

The Talking (and Oversharing) Department

And then, of course, we must address my other lifelong specialty: talking. If there were Olympic medals for excessive conversation and unprompted personal storytelling, I'd be a world champion.

Sharing my life stories on flights, for seven hours, with the poor unsuspecting captive stranger sitting next to me.

They did *not* ask.

But I told them anyway.

It wasn't intentional oversharing; it was simply that my thoughts moved fast and my filter... well... didn't. My brain would spot the tiniest conversational doorway and sprint through it like it was the finish line at Kona.

Finally, the Penny Dropped

So, when I realized my experiences aligned almost perfectly with ADHD, I nearly burst out laughing. ADHD? At my age? Surely that was a childhood thing.

Wrong.

The more I read, the more everything clicked. The fidgeting, the restlessness, the accidents, the impulsive decisions, the forgotten appointments, the half-finished projects (including this memoir, which has taken *only* 25 years), the talking, the catastrophes, the creative obsessions, all of it suddenly made sense.

It wasn't about something being *wrong* with me.

It was about finally understanding why my life has always felt like a fast-paced dance to music no one else could hear.

My brain wasn't broken.

It was simply exuberant. Unconventional. Energetic. A little unruly, perhaps, but bursting with curiosity and creativity.

And after 58 years of wondering what the hell was going on, clarity felt like relief. A warm, gentle exhale.

The Great ADHD Deep Dive

Naturally, I dove headfirst into the rabbit hole of research, which is very ADHD of me. I typed "ADHD in adults" into Google, and 12 hours later, I had learned everything from how dopamine affects motivation to why people like me regularly misplace their keys in the fridge.

(Real example: I once found mine beside the butter. They are currently lost again.)

Every article was like a tiny mirror held up to my past.

Oh, *that's* why I interrupted people mid-sentence.

Oh, *that's* why I start six projects and finish none.

Oh, *that's* why I reorganized my entire living room during a movie.

And yes, the infamous Christmas Eve incident. At 5:30 p.m., 30 minutes before the hardware store was closing, I decided that the living room, dining room, and kitchen needed to be painted *that night*, before hosting Christmas dinner. The dining room, in my infinite wisdom, I chose to paint deep red, a colour known to stimulate appetite but also extremely hard to apply. Six coats later, it looked great. I did not feel great.

Looking back, I honestly marvel that my marriage lasted as long as it did.

It was like discovering the subtitles to my own brain.

Making Peace with the Past

The hardest part wasn't learning what ADHD was.

It was realizing how many years I'd spent blaming myself.

Lazy.

Disorganized.

Too loud.

Too much.

Teachers said I wasn't living up to my potential.

Bosses said I was distractible.

Friends teased me for being accident-prone.

Colleagues rolled their eyes when I talked too much.

I laughed along, because what else could I do? But deep inside, it stung. I thought everyone else had some secret instruction manual I'd somehow missed.

Now I understand the truth.

That little girl who couldn't sit still wasn't being naughty; she was wired to move.

That young woman who made spontaneous decisions wasn't reckless; she was curious and brave.

That 58-year-old finally getting answers wasn't broken; she was simply built with a different rhythm.

And maybe that rhythm is why I trained for and completed 15 full Ironman races and over a hundred other triathlons, including two World Championships. With the proper structure and support, my brain and body can achieve extraordinary things. I'm not unable, just uniquely able.

Learning to Work with My Brain

I've made small but transformative changes. This is a work in progress.

I write *everything* down: grocery lists, reminders, and ideas. I break tasks into tiny steps.

I celebrate finishing one thing instead of grieving the 10 I didn't.

I use timers, apps, and sometimes sheer luck.

I let my mind wander when it wants to. Sometimes, the best ideas arrive during those detours.

My curiosity and hyperfocus allow me to see connections others might miss. It's a gift… when I remember to harness it.

Most importantly, I'm learning to stop apologizing for being "too much." Because maybe "too much" is exactly what made my life so rich, absurd, meaningful, and full of stories worth telling.

Laughing About It

If ADHD has given me anything, it's joy, real, ridiculous joy.

Like the time I boiled the kettle to make tea, forgot about it, vacuumed the entire condo, reorganized half a closet, fell into an internet rabbit hole, then rediscovered the cold kettle six hours later.

Or the time I proudly labelled all my storage boxes... and then promptly forgot what half the labels meant. ("Important Stuff" remains an unsolved mystery.)

Once, these moments frustrated me. Now they amuse me. Because if there's one thing ADHD guarantees, it's that life is *never* boring.

The Realization

Getting diagnosed at 58 wasn't the end of something.

It was the beginning, a homecoming.

It felt like meeting me properly for the first time.

My quirks aren't flaws.

My chaos isn't failure.

My differences aren't deficiencies.

They're features.

I've spent a lifetime trying to fit inside lines that were never designed for me, when I was born with crayons that melted together in the sun, messy, colourful, chaotic, beautiful.

And honestly?

I love my messy masterpiece of a brain.

Closing Note & Disclaimer

Everything I've shared in this chapter comes from my personal experience, the accidents, the impulsive adventures, the late-in-life diagnosis, the relief, the grief, and the unexpected sense of homecoming.

But ADHD shows up differently in everyone.

No two brains spin at the same speed.

No two stories unfold the same way.

I'm not offering medical advice.

I'm offering perspective, one woman's lived experience, toward understanding her own mind after nearly six decades of wondering why she felt "different."

If you think you or someone you love might have ADHD, please talk to a qualified healthcare professional.

Diagnosis, treatment, and support are deeply personal decisions, and you deserve guidance tailored to *your* life, *your* history, and *your* beautiful, complex brain. For more information on supporting those with ADHD, see Appendix B.

And if any part of my story made you feel seen, less alone, or a little more curious about your own wiring?

Then I'm glad you're here.

And I hope you know this:

You are not broken.

You are not behind.

You are not too much.

You are simply wired for a different rhythm,

one that's every bit as extraordinary as mine.

Chapter 16
Learning to Believe

Self-belief isn't lightning. It's layering.

For years, I mistook survival for confidence.

Looking back, I can see the patterns of my life more clearly now: the impulsive leaps, the accidents, the intuition, the strength forged in crisis. The truth had always been there. I just hadn't trusted it.

I had spent a lifetime proving I was capable long before I ever believed it.

Understanding my brain didn't suddenly make me confident, but it gave me clarity: the catastrophes and the creativity, the chaos and the competence, the strange way I always landed on my feet, even when I didn't stick the landing.

With that clarity came a harder realization.

I didn't trust myself.

Not the way other people seemed to trust themselves so effortlessly.

I believed I was "too much" in all the wrong places and "not enough" in all the important ones. I believed the limits other people handed me. I believed the stories my fear whispered, even when the evidence suggested otherwise.

And still, life kept testing those beliefs.

Each time it knocked me down, I stood back up.

Not gracefully.

Not quickly.

But undeniably.

Only later did I recognize what had been happening all along. Without meaning to, I had been building my way back to self-belief, one disaster, one miracle, one messy middle at a time.

It began, not with confidence, but with borrowed belief.

When my coach, Sheldon, told me, “You can still do the Ironman… you’ll just walk the marathon,” he believed in me when I couldn’t. When my home burned down and friends stood beside me, holding a future I couldn’t yet imagine, they carried belief until I could reach for it myself.

Belief, I learned, is often communal.

Then there were the small wins. The unglamorous ones.

One proper meal after the divorce.

One job application after a layoff.

Simply getting out of bed after brain surgery.

They didn’t look like confidence, but they rebuilt the bridge between who I had been and who I was becoming.

I also learned to collect evidence.

Fear is persuasive, and my brain, especially under stress, has a remarkable talent for forgetting its own strengths. So I collected proof: finish-line photos, notes from patients, messages from friends, medical reports showing recovery. When doubt spoke loudly, evidence spoke back.

And then there was my inner critic.

Mine has a name: Gertrude. She specializes in worst-case scenarios.

"You'll mess this up."

"You can't do this."

"This will end terribly."

Now, when she shows up, I thank her politely for her concern and inform her that I won't be calling her back. Turning fear into comedy shrinks it to a manageable size.

Perhaps the most important shift was learning to separate feeling from fact.

Feeling: *I won't survive this.*

Fact: *I always have.*

Feeling: *My marriage ended, so I must be unlovable.*

Fact: *My capacity to love remains intact.*

Feeling: *Losing my job means I failed.*

Fact: *Thirteen years of showing up still counts.*

That distinction changed everything.

Along the way, I noticed how much the people around me

mattered. Friends held me up after the fire and supported me through cancer and loss, brought me home after surgeries and took care of me. Coaches who expected more of me, and were right. People who stretched my sense of what was possible simply by living their lives out loud.

This truth became clear: We rise by proximity.

With this understanding, I finally learned to speak to myself the way I speak to people I love. I would never tell a patient they were too much. I would never tell a friend they were failing. So why had I spent decades saying those things to myself?

Gradually, I realized that self-belief is built through language.

The gentler the language, the better.

Self-belief isn't magic. It isn't a lightning strike.

It's maintenance, a relationship you return to daily.

It is rebuilt after detours.

Strengthened after heartbreak.

Reclaimed after miracles.

So when life asks me now: *Who are you?*

I answer more honestly than I used to.

I am someone who survives.

I am someone who tries again. And I am someone who is finally believing in herself... most of the time.

Self-belief is an evolving process. I still have moments of uncertainty and doubt. It still needs tending. But with practice, it gets easier.

In Appendix C, I've shared the lessons I return to when mine feels shaky.

I am not always fearless. I am not always certain.

But I no longer wait for someone else to tell me who I am.

Chapter 17
Resilience: Training for the Hard Things

"You never know how strong you are until being strong is your only choice."
Bob Marley

I'm not entirely sure where my resilience came from, but I suspect it's less a single source and more a long, chaotic recipe.

Some of it came from sheer survival: the surgeries, the house fire, the divorce, the breast cancer, the broken bones, and the layoffs.

Some of it came from people: friends who showed up with casseroles and humour, neighbours who reviewed insurance policies, colleagues who walked beside me through endless hospital corridors, my family, who poured Baileys and played Peggy Lee when my condo burned down.

And some of it came from a quiet, stubborn knowing that eventually, not immediately, not neatly, things were going to be okay.

Resilience, it turns out, works the same way belief does: not in flashes, but in layers built under pressure.

Over time, with each catastrophe and comeback, I didn't just become more resilient. I became more grateful. More aware of how fragile life is, and how strong we can be.

Triathlon training had a lot to do with it, too. Ironman didn't just give me muscles; it trained my mind to problem-solve under pressure, to treat challenges like races: the preparation, the doing, the suffering, the recovery.

When cancer came, that training came with me.

Training for Life

I can still feel the coldness of the doctor's office right before she said it.

"It's breast cancer."

For a moment, time stalled. The hum of fluorescent lights grew louder. My breath caught somewhere between my chest and my throat.

I whispered to myself: *You've faced hard things before. You can do this.*

Stepping out of the hospital in that heaviness, I saw a man walking down the street wearing a sweatshirt that read: ***"I HATE RUBBER BOOTS."*** He was wearing rubber boots.

I laughed out loud. A ridiculous little flare of humour in the dark.

And deep down, I knew I could do this, because by then I'd spent years in what I now think of as the resilience gym.

Ironman, especially, is not just a physical sport. It's a psychological experiment you sign up for voluntarily.

Cold, dark mornings.

Muscles screaming.

Rain that feels personal.

I remember one particularly brutal long run. I stood at the end of my driveway, already soaked, every cell in my body lobbying for the couch.

A coach's words floated back to me:

"Resilience is built on the days you don't want to train."

So, I went. One stubborn step at a time.

Those races taught me a cycle:

Preparation → Endurance → Struggle → Breakthrough → Recovery.

Standing at the exit of the hospital with a new diagnosis lodged in my chest, I recognized the rhythm.

Different terrain. Higher stakes. Still a race.

Race Day, Redefined

Surgery day felt like stepping up to a starting line I never signed up for.

The hospital was bright and icy, the kind of light that makes everything feel too real. Instead of a wetsuit, I wore a hospital gown. Instead of a race bib, I had a plastic wristband.

Because it was COVID, no one could come in with me. No family in the waiting room. No hand to squeeze.

But I carried something else instead: my people.

Thank goodness for Patrick, who walked with me to the hospital entrance and made me laugh with his ridiculous but thoughtful story about a dragon who finds a lump under her wing.

Text messages buzzed in one after another:

"We're with you."

"You've got this."

"Pretend we're all right there holding your hands... six feet away, of course."

I smiled at that one. Somehow, humour travels better than anything across six feet of air.

Walking toward the operating room, I realized: resilience isn't about facing things alone. It's about knowing who is quietly standing with you, even when they can't physically be there.

The Slow Work of Recovery

When I woke up after surgery, everything hurt.

Recovery wasn't glamorous. It wasn't an inspirational montage from a movie. It was slow, boring, sometimes painful, and occasionally ridiculous.

On some days, lifting my arm a few centimetres higher than the day before felt like crossing an Ironman finish line. On others, simply getting out of bed and into clean pyjamas was the win.

I'd always thought resilience was toughness.

But recovery taught me that resilience is also softness:

letting people help.

letting myself rest.

letting tears come when they needed to.

So, I let myself cry. At the kitchen table. In the shower. In bed at 3 a.m., staring at the ceiling and wondering what my life would look like a year from then.

Crying wasn't a failure. It was a release. Another kind of training.

Supported by a Six-Foot Radius of Love

Even with physical distance, my people showed up.

Meals left on my doorstep.

Flowers dropped off like little bursts of colour.

Neighbours waving through windows.

Friends scheduling indoor bike ride video calls, so I didn't disappear into my own head.

Colleagues sending cards and messages.

Family calling from afar.

They didn't need to be in the same room to make me feel held.

I realized then that community is one of the secret ingredients of resilience.

Exercise made me strong.

Triathlon made me tough.

But my people made me brave.

The Mindset Shift That Changed Everything

Resilience isn't about pretending everything is fine. It's about choosing how you'll move through the mess.

In the quiet days between appointments and recovery naps, my mind wanted to spiral:

Why me?

What if it comes back?

What if I can't do the things I love again?

But somewhere between all of my previous challenges, a new question had begun to form:

"What can this teach me?"

Not in a toxic-positivity, "everything happens for a reason" way. But in a curious way.

What strength am I building here?

What part of me is being reshaped?

How might this help me help someone else later?

Slowly, sometimes so slowly I didn't notice, it happened.

I became less afraid of the next wave. Not because I

assumed it would be easy, but because I had evidence I could survive the hard things.

This challenge didn't just test me. It remade me.

My Resilience Toolkit (So Far)

Over time, I've realized resilience isn't one thing.

It's a toolbox.

Mine includes:

Movement

Walking, biking, swimming, or stretching on the floor. Movement reminds me I still live in my body, not just my head. Even five minutes counts.

Breathing

A few slow, deliberate breaths when my mind starts sprinting ahead of me. Breathing pulls me back into the present moment.

Writing

Journaling or dumping worries onto paper so they don't rattle around my brain all night. Once they're written down, they feel more manageable.

Crying

No apologies. Crying doesn't mean I'm weak. Tears from sadness, anger, or frustration carry stress hormones, which may be why crying often leaves you lighter. Tears of joy are simpler: mostly salt and water. Different tears, different jobs. Either way, it's just the body doing a bit of housekeeping for the heart.

Humour (a.k.a. my emotional flotation device)

If I can laugh, even a tiny, snorty laugh or a ridiculous giggle, it means I'm still in there. Laughter loosens the grip of pain and gives my nervous system a brief exhale. In dark moments, even micro-sparks of joy matter. Bonus points for tears and crossed-leg situations.

Community

Letting friends in. Saying yes to help. Allowing people to carry pieces of the load when mine gets too heavy.

Boundaries

Protecting my energy. Saying no without overexplaining. Choosing rest without guilt.

Purpose

Remembering that helping others, sharing my story, or making even a small difference grounds me when everything else feels unsteady.

Resilience means having ways to gather yourself back up.

Outside assistance

I've learned to reach for support, sitting with a counsellor to untangle what I couldn't do alone, using a light-therapy lamp through dark winters, and working with a wonderful life coach, Timea, who helped me see forward when my own vision felt cloudy. None of this meant I was broken. It meant I was paying attention. Seeking professional support didn't weaken my resilience; it strengthened it. Asking for help isn't a detour; it's often the most direct path through.

Quiet Truths I've Learned

- Resilience isn't about how much you can endure.
  It's about how willing you are to receive support, rest when needed, and trust that rebuilding is part of the process.
- Sometimes, the greatest strength is found in our gentlest moments, when we allow ourselves to be human, vulnerable, and open to healing.
- Resilience isn't about bouncing back to who you were before, but growing into who you're becoming through each experience.

Questions to Ponder

- Where in your life are you being asked to soften instead of push?
- Who helps you feel most like yourself when things fall apart?
- What small act of self-kindness could you offer yourself the next time you're struggling?
- When was the last time you allowed yourself to accept help, and how did it feel?

✨ RESILIENCE CHECKLIST

For the moments when life wobbles, tilts, or tries to knock you flat.

- ✔ Celebrate one tiny win.
- ✔ Move your body, even gently.
- ✔ Breathe slowly and on purpose.
- ✔ Cry without apology.
- ✔ Laugh if you can. Any version counts.
- ✔ Ask: "Is this a feeling or a fact?"
- ✔ Name your inner critic, then dismiss them.
- ✔ Look for proof of what you've already handled.
- ✔ Identify one controllable next step.
- ✔ Reach out to one person.
- ✔ Seek outside assistance.
- ✔ Choose kindness over perfection.

Chapter 18
Being Competitive... Or Not

I stopped racing other people the day
I learned how to finish my own race.

"Paula, you absolutely have to stop running."

I had been competing in triathlons for about 15 years when I heard the words every athlete fears. After years of injuries and stubbornly pushing through pain, because that's what we do, often against all reasonable medical advice, I was finally diagnosed with severe arthritis in my ankles (caused by the abnormally high growth hormone years ago, and possibly a "little" bit of wear and tear).

The specialist didn't sugarcoat anything.

"If you don't stop running, you may not be able to walk by the time you're 60."

To be honest, I've never loved running, and running did not like me. It was always so painful and caused chronic injuries. But not being able to walk was definitely not on my list of life goals. I left the appointment devastated. Running wasn't just a sport; it was what got me to the finish line. To make matters worse, I was supposed to race an Ironman in exactly three weeks.

I told my coach, Sheldon, assuming he would confirm what I already believed: that my Ironman days were over.

Instead, without missing a beat, he shrugged and said,

"Well... why don't you just walk the marathon?"

Walk? The marathon?

That was either the most ridiculous or the most brilliant idea I'd ever heard. But when faced with surrender or insanity, I usually choose insanity. It's more fun. So, that night, I went out for my first official "speed walk."

I must have looked like a very determined duck preparing for takeoff, arms pumping, hips swinging. I'm sure I looked ridiculous.

The next day, every single joint in my body complained loudly.

Possibly in multiple languages.

Clearly, something needed to change.

So, I invented my own technique. I affectionately called it *Paula's Power Glide*.

It was inspired by cross-country skiing... if cross-country skiing had no skis, no poles, and no snow... so, really, nothing like cross-country skiing. Less hip action than speed walking. I pumped my arms enthusiastically and shuffled my feet at a pace that suggested I was fleeing an uncomfortable social interaction.

And surprisingly?

It worked.

In fact, I began walking fast enough to pass actual runners.

One evening, during one of my newly perfected "power glides," I was striding along the Waterfront Trail at dusk, deeply invested in my own athletic heroism, when I sensed someone behind me. You know that feeling, someone gaining on you, closing in.

Without being too obvious, I peeked behind me. A shadow. Definitely a runner.

Well then.

If they wanted to pass me, they'd *have to earn it.*

I pumped my arms harder. Increased the cadence of my feet. Heart rate soared into the 180s. Sweat poured. My breathing sounded like I was auditioning for a wildlife documentary.

But I was determined: I would outwalk this runner.

Why wouldn't they just pass me already?

Finally, when I was seconds from collapsing into a melodramatic heap, I looked back again.

There was nobody there.

Not a single person.

The runner I was valiantly battling?

My own shadow.

🏃 Reflections

- Often, our toughest competitor is ourselves.
- Adaptation can lead to unexpected strengths and new paths, even after a setback or loss.
- Letting go of external expectations can help us discover our own definition of success.
- Humour and creativity can transform even the most difficult challenges into memorable experiences.

💭 Questions to Ask Yourself

- Have you ever realized you were competing against your own expectations or limitations?
- How do you respond when life forces you to adapt your goals or methods?
- What does finishing your own race mean to you?
- In what ways can you bring humour or creativity to your personal challenges?

Chapter 19
The First Brave Step

If triathlon taught me anything, it's this:
your real strength appears when you choose to begin,
not when you cross the finish line.

People often ask me, "Who can do a triathlon?"

For years, my answer was simple: "If I can do a triathlon, anyone can do one."

Then I'd back that up with "If you have two arms and two legs, you can do a triathlon."

But truthfully, triathlon is for far more people than we imagine. I've seen athletes with diverse abilities, including those who may not fit the traditional view of an athlete, compete and conquer their own challenges. It's a sport that welcomes people of all abilities, encouraging everyone to join and feel inspired.

That's when I understood something important.

Triathlon isn't about perfection.

It's about possibility.

Somewhere in that season, something else shifted, too.

I stopped measuring myself against everyone else and started paying attention to what was actually happening in my body and in my life.

The only person I really needed to be competitive with was myself. (Unless, of course, I was racing my own shadow... which probably says more about my personality than my fitness.)

I didn't stop being competitive.

I just started enjoying the part where I was still alive and moving.

And before this sounds like motivational theory, let me be clear: I didn't think my way into a gentler definition of success. I lived it.

I power-walked to multiple Ironman finish lines, including World Championships, sprint and Olympic-distance races. I did it not by being faster than anyone else, but by staying in my own lane long enough to finish.

If triathlon isn't for you, that's more than okay.

The point was never the sport.

It was the spark.

Swimming lanes. Bridge clubs. Pickleball. Walking groups. Book clubs. Choirs. Volunteering. Community gardens. Anything that pulls you out of your head and toward other people.

Because passion expands us, but community changes us. And more often than not, it isn't the activity that transforms a life. It's the people you meet while doing it.

For me, triathlon began at a moment when my life cracked open.

Not from inspiration.

From betrayal.

When I realized my boyfriend was cheating on me, I knew I needed somewhere to put the energy before I completely gave up on myself. Around that same time, a patient mentioned she was training for a triathlon.

Something lit up.

I didn't become an athlete because I was ready.

I became one because I needed somewhere to put my pain.

I said yes before I felt brave.

Over the years, I've noticed how often transformation begins this way. So many people I know didn't change because life was going well. They changed because something broke. A loss. A diagnosis. A betrayal. A moment they could no longer ignore. The tipping point is rarely gentle. But it can be catalytic.

And I didn't do it alone.

A couple of races in, after some sprints, some tragic transitions, and finish-line photos that made me look like I'd survived a natural disaster, I met Inga.

"You should join the Clydesdales," she said.

"The who?"

I pictured majestic horses clip-clopping through transition zones.

She laughed. “The Clydesdales. Women over 150 pounds, and men over 200. Strong athletes who don’t look like magazine models, but who show up with grit and heart.”

I’m 5′11″. I’ve been over 150 pounds since I was about eight years old. I will likely remain over 150 pounds for the rest of my natural life.

This group was basically built for me.

At training camp, everything clicked.

No judgment.

No apologies.

No shrinking yourself to fit someone else’s idea of what you’re supposed to be.

Just people who trained hard, laughed loudly, and cheered wildly.

Upon reflection, I understand why that mattered so much.

It reminded me, in the best possible way, of what happened when I was eight years old: being moved into a remedial class. At the time, it felt like failure. But that classroom gave me space. Room to breathe. A place where I could keep up, participate, even excel.

The Clydesdales did the same thing.

For the first time in sport, I wasn’t struggling to measure up. I was competitive within the group, and that mattered. Feeling capable made me want to stay. Made me want to try, and to get better.

Belonging didn’t make me complacent.

It made me brave.

Later, I joined the Toronto Triathlon Club. Between the Clydesdales and TTC, I didn't just become an athlete.

I found community and belonging.

This is what I understand most clearly: triathlon didn't change my life because of distances, gear, or finish times. It changed my life because I said yes to it, and because I didn't have to do it alone.

Everything else was learnable. Adjustable. Forgiving.

It was never really about the sport, but about what it invited me to discover. It taught me to start before certainty arrived, to keep moving when everything protested, to laugh through the chaos, to accept a hand when mine was shaking, to trust the smallest steps, and to believe I could stretch farther than I imagined.

The lesson that stays with me most: strength doesn't wait at the finish line. It rises the moment you choose to try.

Maybe you're realizing how much lighter hard things become when someone walks beside you. Or maybe there's a small step you've been circling, not because you're incapable, but because you haven't yet allowed yourself to take it.

If any part of this stirs curiosity about triathlon or any other brave beginning, there are plenty of books, coaches, websites, and opinions ready to teach you the mechanics. But if you're ready for something simpler, consider signing up for a beginner-friendly event or joining a group that welcomes newcomers. Those first small actions can turn inspiration into motion.

And remember, this isn't really about triathlon. It's about listening when something inside you whispers, *What if?* and letting yourself answer, *Maybe*.

If this chapter offers anything, I hope it's this: beginnings don't ask for confidence. They ask for courage, the kind that grows with every step you take.

How to Make the Process FUN
(Highly Recommended)

🌟 Treat workouts like mini-adventures.

🚴 Name your bike (mandatory) and decorate it to make it yours. Mine has flowers. Many flowers... 🌸🌸🌸

🏃 Make a training playlist. (Note: no headphones in races.)

🧜 Celebrate the awkward moments—they become the best stories.

👯 Bring a friend. It's far less daunting, and training is better when it's social.

💗 Remember: nobody cares about your pace.

🦄 Appreciate the volunteers, especially the ones dressed as pink unicorns. 😉

🏅 Smile with your arms in the air at the finish line. Your photos will thank you.

😄 Finishing a race is magical. It's emotion, relief, pride, and transformation.

✨ You don't have to win. You just have to start.

Chapter 20
The Things That Saved Me

Meaning unfolds, but it takes time.

Looking back over the past 25 years, I realize that many of the most astonishing, absurd, serendipitous, and miraculous things began because of a brain tumour. Honestly, if this were fiction, an editor might send it back with a polite note saying, "Love your imagination, but please choose a lane."

But life doesn't choose lanes.

It swerves, twists, and turns between plot points, and occasionally hops a curb for dramatic effect.

Sometimes I wonder if the tumour's earliest whisper was that strange spark in my head that said, very casually, "Why don't you try a triathlon?" I'd been quite content being horizontal. The tumour had been growing long before anyone named it. Long before I knew it was rewriting my life. It lines up perfectly with the moment I abruptly stopped being a couch potato and started racing through life like someone auditioning for a Nike commercial.

If I hadn't had that mysterious surge of energy from the excess growth hormone...

If I hadn't developed endurance that made no sense...

Pull one thread, and the whole tapestry rearranges itself into a completely different (and beige) life.

Would I have ever stepped onto the starting line of my first Ironman?

That's where I met my future ex-husband. A chapter that mattered, even if the marriage didn't endure.

Before any of that, I spent years being told it was "all in my head." Technically, yes, just not in the way they meant.

One doctor missed that my growth hormone levels were abnormally high. If she'd recognized it, I never would've raced. But she didn't. So I did.

The tumour kept fueling me, and I kept getting stronger, faster, more capable. Every win made me train harder, placing me directly on the path to people who would change my life.

A year after diagnosis and surgery, I returned to triathlon.

That comeback led to an interview. The interview led to an article. The article reached a family in the darkest moment of their lives.

They said yes to organ donation.

That single yes gave my friend and several others, more time. More birthdays. More ordinary moments that suddenly mattered more.

That ripple still stops me in my tracks.

Triathlon handed me far more than finish lines. It gave me

family disguised as friends, strangers who became lifelines, and a community that showed up exactly when I needed it most. I met Doug at a finish line years before his brain tumour needed my support. I met Esther, who helped me find a job, and later, I helped her with her own pituitary and acromegaly journey.

So many threads. So many lives woven together. None of this could've been planned.

And then came the sequence of events I truly never expected, the chain reaction triggered by my divorce.

I needed a roommate. The roommate came with, let's call it, chaotic optimism in the pantry: boxes of batteries lovingly and catastrophically reorganized. The kind of organization that seems harmless until it sparks a large-scale science experiment.

That's how I ended up watching my life burn down.

I remember thinking: a rare hemorrhaging brain tumour, lightning, and an earthquake weren't enough? Now we're trying fire?

And yet, even that catastrophe carried a strange grace.

What rose from the ashes was brighter than what had burned. Something I never could've afforded. A fresh start disguised as drywall and paint.

My own phoenix rising.

While writing this memoir, tracing every twist and tremor of my life, my brain delivered one more surprise: I was diagnosed with ADHD.

In my fifties.

While writing a memoir.

About plot twists.

You truly cannot make this sh*t up.

Suddenly it all made sense: the way my brain sparks, the way memories braid themselves into unexpected patterns, the way I leap between thoughts like stepping stones, except the stones are floating, out of order, and occasionally on fire, and somehow, I still land (mostly) upright.

This is how my brain works: fast, curious, connective, creative, and, let's be honest, occasionally chaotic.

And I'm proud of it. Unashamedly, loudly, colourfully proud.

For a long time, I believed the tumour and the excess growth hormone gave me superpowers. But when they were gone, and I got faster and stronger anyway, I finally understood: Maybe I'd been capable all along.

The tumour may have lit the match.

But I carried the fire.

When I step back and look at everything, the tumour, the heartbreaks, the fire, the cancer, the crashes, the divorce, and now ADHD, it almost feels implausible.

A Bridget Jones-meets-Forrest Gump real-life sitcom with slapstick, drama, and the occasional miracle.

But beneath the absurdity is something rock-solid:

I wouldn't rewrite my whole story, even knowing how hard

some of it would be.

Not the fear. Not the mayhem. Not the moments that brought me to my knees.

Would I delete some scenes? Absolutely. Some things were just painful.

Still, it changed me. I'm stronger, softer, and braver now. I can sit with someone in their hardest moments and say, *"You are not alone in this. There is still hope, even if you can't feel it yet."*

I do not survive because I'm extraordinary. I survive because people hold me steady, and humour keeps me afloat. I survive because I keep taking the next step.

If I can laugh, even through tears and at myself, it means I'm still in there.

This stubborn, wildly wired brain of mine has always been determined to turn chaos into connection.

In the end, it wasn't just the tumour that saved me. It was every messy, miraculous moment, and the people who walked beside me that revealed the strength that had been mine all along.

A Final Letter to You, Dear Reader

Thank you for walking with me through the wild, crooked, hilarious, heartbreaking maze of my life. If you've made it to this final page, I hope that somewhere between the surgeries and the fire, between the triathlons and the tears, you found a piece of yourself reflected here.

If I've learned anything, it's that sometimes our lives are too wild to be plausible and too meaningful to be accidents. The challenges I once thought would defeat me didn't disappear, but they did change me. Over time, they revealed strength, connection, and growth I never could have predicted.

We spend so much of our lives believing we must be fearless before we begin, healed before we try, and confident before we leap. My life is proof that this simply isn't true. I wasn't ready for most of what came my way, but somehow, each time, I took the next step anyway. You don't need all the answers. You only need permission to begin where you are.

If you're standing at the edge of something right now, an ending, a beginning, a dream you're afraid to want, borrow belief when you need it. Let people hold you when your legs shake. Speak to yourself as if you are someone worth rooting for.

Wherever you are in your own story, I'm cheering for you. Not because life won't hit hard sometimes, but because I believe in your capacity to meet it, in your own way, and in your own time.

Before we part, I want to say this gently: any meaning I describe here is personal, not universal, and never a requirement.

I don't believe suffering guarantees growth or that pain exists for a reason. When I write about hope, resilience, or life happening for me, I'm describing a choice I made, not a rule I expect anyone else to follow. Take what feels useful. Leave what doesn't. Trust that your own way of making sense of things, if and when you choose to, is enough.

If these pages kept you company, comforted you, or reminded you of your own strength, I hope you'll consider sharing this with a friend or someone who might appreciate my journey and reflections. Stories travel farther when we pass them along. Your voice may be the one that reaches someone who needs it next.

I'd also love to hear from you. You can find me at **paulastories.com** or connect with me on social media. You're always welcome.

I'm looking forward to whatever my next chapter brings, ideally with fewer surgeries and natural disasters.

Whatever comes, I'll meet it the same way I've met everything else: imperfectly, curiously, and never alone.

I hope you will too.

With love and hope,

Paula

Acknowledgements

This book took 25 years to write, and I did not do it alone.

To Angela, who handed me a journal 25 years ago and said, *"You should write your book."*

This is me, finally listening.

To my dear friends, neighbours, and colleagues, those who carried me through illness, heartbreak, uncertainty, and reinvention, thank you. You showed up with meals, messages, laughter, and patience. You sat beside me in the mess and cheered wildly at the finish lines. You reminded me, again and again, that I was never running solo.

A special thank you to June, Ann, Angie, Jill, Patrick, and to the many others I hold close, even if space prevents me from naming you all here.

To my triathlon and swim coaches, thank you for believing before I did. To the physios, massage therapists and chiropractors who worked on my injured body more than I care to remember, I am grateful. And to Lisa Bentley, thank you for that early encouragement in sport that helped me see what was possible long before I felt ready.

To Fr. Dan and Fr. Tony, with gratitude for the miracles you helped set in motion.

I wish to honour the late Dr. Fred Gentili, an extraordinary neurosurgeon whose passion, skill, and compassion saved countless lives, including mine. His passing in January 2022, after his own battle with a brain tumour, was a profound loss. I remain deeply grateful for the care, dedication, and humanity that gave me a future.

In memory of Barbara Turnbull, writer, advocate, and fierce champion for spinal cord research, accessibility, organ donation, and so many causes that mattered. Thank you for proving that words can move systems, and stories can change the world.

To Samantha and Simar, thank you for helping bring this long-held dream to life. To the author community who welcomed me with open arms, your encouragement, wisdom, and generosity made this journey lighter and far more joyful.

To Dr. Ezzat, Lori, Deanna, Jill, Mark, and everyone living with or advocating for awareness of acromegaly, thank you for your tireless work, your voices, and your determination to ensure others are diagnosed and treated sooner than many of us were.

An Uncomfortable but Necessary Thank You

To the teacher who doubted me: Your words stayed with me longer than you realized. They didn't have the effect you intended; instead, they became my motivation.

To the person who cheated: Thank you for the heartbreak that led me to my first triathlon. That unexpected turn changed everything.

And to my ex-husband, thank you for the years you stood

by me. Thank you also for encouraging my triathlon hobby, which became a lifestyle, a personality trait, and a bit of an obsession. Even endings can hold gratitude.

Without these people, my life might have turned out differently. It wasn't their kindness, but the way they changed my path. Sometimes, the people who challenge us most push us toward the life we're meant to live.

About the Author

Paula Johnson is a registered nurse, endurance athlete, speaker, and author who believes that resilience is something we build, not something we're given.

Originally from England, Paula immigrated to Canada at 24, continuing her career in healthcare while navigating a life marked by unexpected detours, illness, loss, reinvention, and more than a few memorable cycling mishaps. Along the way, she discovered that belief is not innate; it grows in small steps, through borrowed courage, humour, and the support of community.

Today, she shares her story to encourage others: You don't have to feel ready to begin; you just have to begin. Known for her candour, warmth, and ability to find lightness even in adversity, she writes and speaks for those standing at the edge of change, searching for hope, strength, and possibility.

Her audiences include women navigating major life changes, healthcare and patient advocacy communities, athletes facing change, corporate teams under pressure, and anyone standing on the cusp of a new beginning.

She lives in Toronto, Canada, and can usually be found moving: power walking, cycling, swimming, paddleboarding, or cheering someone else on as they take their next brave step.

Let's stay connected!

Instagram: @paulajstories

LinkedIn: https://www.linkedin.com/in/paula-johnson-2820b61b/

Website: https://www.paulastories.com

Appendix A
What Is Acromegaly?

Acromegaly is a hormonal condition that occurs when the pituitary gland produces too much growth hormone (GH), often due to a benign tumour, known as a pituitary adenoma. This excess GH stimulates the liver to produce insulin-like growth factor 1 (IGF-1), which promotes growth in various tissues and organs.

Acromegaly is notoriously difficult to diagnose because its symptoms develop gradually and can be mistaken for other conditions. Many patients experience significant delays before receiving a correct diagnosis. Education, awareness, and patient advocacy are crucial to help healthcare professionals and the public recognize signs earlier, leading to quicker diagnosis, successful treatment and improved patient outcomes.

Acromegaly symptoms can change the way some body parts look. Common visible changes can include:

- Thick ears and lips.
- A broad nose.
- Enlarged hands and feet.
- A jutting brow or jaw.

- Gaps between teeth.
- An enlarged tongue.
- An expanded rib cage that may cause the chest to have a round shape.

Skin changes in acromegaly may include acne, skin tags, thickened or oily skin, and swelling under the skin.

Most often, people with acromegaly don't have every possible body change. And because the changes come on slowly, they may take years to notice.

How does acromegaly affect the body? Beyond visible changes, too much GH and IGF-1 affect many organs and systems. Specific effects include:

- **Dental health.** Acromegaly can cause an unusually large jaw and spacing between the teeth. People may notice gaps forming between teeth, bite changes or teeth that don't line up correctly. The tongue also may enlarge, leading to speech and breathing problems. Regular dental care is important for managing these oral changes.
- **Reproductive and sexual health.** Excess growth hormone can affect reproductive health. In men, acromegaly may lead to erectile dysfunction, reduced libido and low testosterone. Enlargement of soft tissues also may occur, but sexual issues are usually due to hormonal imbalance rather than physical enlargement.

- **Voice changes.** Thickening of tissues in the vocal cords and throat can make the voice deeper or hoarser over time. Some people also notice snoring or changes in speech.

Early symptoms of acromegaly may be subtle, such as changes in ring or shoe size. As the condition progresses, other common symptoms can include:

- Vision troubles, including loss of side vision.
- More sweating and body odor than is typical.
- Fatigue and low energy.
- Headaches.
- Joint pain.
- Sleep problems, including sleep apnea.

Complications

If left untreated, acromegaly can lead to serious health issues, including:

- Cardiovascular problems: Increased risk of heart disease, hypertension, and enlarged heart.
- Diabetes: Elevated blood sugar levels can lead to type 2 diabetes.
- Joint issues: Osteoarthritis and other joint problems may develop.
- Increased risk of certain cancers, including breast, thyroid and colorectal cancer.

Treatment Options

Treatment for acromegaly aims to reduce GH levels and alleviate symptoms. Common approaches include:

- Surgery: Removing the tumour from the pituitary gland is often the first line of treatment.
- Medications: Drugs such as somatostatin analogs can help lower GH production.
- Radiation therapy: This may be used if surgery is not possible or if the tumour remains after surgery.

Source: Acromegaly - Symptoms and causes - Mayo Clinic

Appendix B
How to Support Someone With ADHD (From Someone Who Lives With It)

And because understanding my own brain changed everything, I want to share what I wish the people around me had known.

If you're reading this and suspect that someone you love might have ADHD, or you already know that they do, here's what I wish I could tell every partner, parent, friend, coworker, and well-meaning stranger in the produce aisle.

Support doesn't need to be dramatic.

It doesn't need to be perfect.

It just needs to be understanding.

These are the things that have meant the most to me, and to so many others who live with neurodivergent (I prefer the term neurodifferent) brains:

1. Believe Them.

ADHD isn't an excuse; it's an explanation. When someone says they're struggling with focus, time, emotional regulation, or overwhelm, trust that it's real.

Validation is powerful medicine.

2. Be Patient With the "Invisible" Challenges.

The forgotten appointments, the overflowing inbox, the dishes that somehow reproduce overnight, none of this reflects laziness or apathy.

It reflects a brain that files information unpredictably.

3. Offer Clarity, Not Criticism.

Clear plans, written instructions, and concrete expectations aren't condescending. They're scaffolding.

ADHD brains thrive when the path is visible.

4. Break Things Into Smaller Pieces.

A big task can feel like standing at the base of Everest.

But "Let's do the first step together"?

That can be a lifeline.

5. Encourage Their Strengths.

Creativity, hyperfocus, empathy, problem solving: ADHD comes bundled with brilliance.

Help them see it. Reflect it back to them. Celebrate it.

6. Make Space for Their Way of Being.

Some people need movement. Some need timers. Some need quiet. Some need disarray.

The goal isn't to make them function like *you*.

It's to help them function like *themselves*.

7. Ask, "What Helps You Most?"

The question itself is love.

You don't have to guess, just ask.

8. Don't Take Forgetfulness Personally.

Missed texts or birthdays aren't a reflection of love.

They're a reflection of how ADHD filters information.

When in doubt: assume affection, not intention.

9. Offer Gentle Accountability, If Invited.

Not nagging. Not managing.

Partnering.

Reminders, shared checklists: these can be game-changers.

10. Celebrate Progress, Not Perfection.

ADHD isn't something to cure.

It's something to understand, support, and honour.

Even small steps deserve recognition.

Appendix C
BELIEVE – A practical way to build self-belief when life keeps testing you

---

I didn't set out to create a framework. I set out to survive.

This emerged slowly through injury, loss, reinvention, and the quiet decision to keep going anyway.

Looking back, these were the steps I returned to again and again.

B – Borrow belief until yours grows

Self-belief doesn't always start inside you. Sometimes it starts around you.

A coach who says, *You can still do this, just differently.*

Friends who stand beside you when you can't see a future yet.

People who hold belief for you until you're ready to take it back.

Borrowed belief counts.

E – Embrace micro-wins

Self-belief doesn't arrive in big, cinematic moments.

It grows in millimetres.

Two minutes of physio after surgery.

One decent meal after heartbreak.

One job application sent.

One day you simply show up.

Micro-wins rebuild trust between who you were and who you're becoming.

L – Look for evidence

Fear has a short memory for success and a vivid imagination for failure.

So I keep proof:

- finish-line photos
- notes from patients
- messages from friends
- medical reports showing recovery
- encouragement I'd otherwise dismiss

When doubt speaks, evidence answers.

I – Interrupt your inner critic

My inner critic has a name. (Gertrude.)

She predicts catastrophe with impressive confidence.

"You'll mess this up."

"This is going to be crap."

"This will end badly."

I acknowledge her enthusiasm and decline the audition.

Humour shrinks fear faster than argument ever did.

E – Examine feeling versus fact

Feelings are real, but they aren't always true.

Feeling: *"I won't survive this."*

Fact: *"I always have."*

Feeling: *"This ending means I failed."*

Fact: *"Endings don't erase effort, love, or growth."*

Learning to separate the two became one of my most reliable tools.

V – Value your expanders

Some people stretch your sense of what's possible just by existing.

Friends who've survived what you're facing.

Coaches who expect more of you than you expect of yourself.

Strangers who quietly model courage.

We don't rise alone.

We rise by proximity.

E – Encourage yourself like someone you love

I would never speak to a patient or a friend the way I once spoke to myself.

So I changed the language:

less judgment;

more patience;

a gentler tone when things go wrong.

Self-belief is built through words, especially the ones you use when no one else is listening.

Closing Note

Self-belief isn't fixed. It develops through practice, imperfectly, over time.

And it strengthens each time you choose to return to it.

thank you

Thank you for reading my book!

Dear Reader,

You made it! Thank you for walking with me through the wild, crooked, hilarious, heartbreaking maze of my life.

If I could ask a small favour: if this book inspired or encouraged you, would you consider leaving a review on Amazon or Goodreads? Your words not only brighten my day but also help others discover this story. You never know, your review could be the spark that helps another person find hope, strength, and possibility.

With gratitude,

Paula

MY GIFT TO YOU

I am so glad you're here!

As my gift to you, get FREE Access to the Audiobook of The Brain Tumour That Saved Me and other bonus content by scanning the QR Code below or visiting

http://paulastories.com

www.ingramcontent.com/pod-product-compliance
Lightning Source LLC
LaVergne TN
LVHW011815200926
848484LV00005B/1200
* 9 7 8 1 9 9 7 7 7 5 6 1 4 *